creating
contemporary
jewelry with
silver, gold,
copper, brass
& more

mixed metals

melinda barta
& danielle fox

INTERWEAVE.
interweavestore.com

editor
KATRINA LOVING

photography
JOE COCA

cover & interior design
PAMELA NORMAN

photo styling
PAM CHAVEZ

illustration
SASHA MARTYNCHUK

technical editing
JAMIE HOGSETT

technical illustration
ANN SWANSON, GAYLE FORD,
DUSTIN WEDEKIND

production
KATHERINE JACKSON

Interweave Press LLC
201 East Fourth Street
Loveland, CO 80537-5655 USA
interweavestore.com

Printed in China by Asia Pacific Offset.

Library of Congress Cataloging-in-Publication Data
Fox, Danielle.
  Mixed metals : creating contemporary jewelry with silver,
gold,copper, brass, and more / Danielle Fox, Melinda Barta,
authors.
      p. cm.

  Includes index.
  ISBN 978-1-59668-092-0 (pbk.)
  1. Jewelry making. 2. Metal-work.
        I. Barta, Melinda A. II. Title.

TT212.F687 2009
745.594'2--dc22
                        2008051116

10 9 8 7 6 5 4 3 2 1

acknowledgments

thank you. First, we thank Jason and Nicolai for their never-ending support and patience during the many nights and weekends we spent beading, writing, and researching for this book—time that might otherwise have been spent with them in the Colorado outdoors. We promise to take a break from beading soon (but to warn you, not for too long)! Thank you to our family and friends—especially Danielle's parents, Annie and Den Fox, and Melinda's parents, Ron and Jean Barta—we couldn't have taken on such a large endeavor without your love and support.

Thank you to the editors, designers, illustrators, and photographers who made this book possible, including Nancy Arndt, Marlene Blessing, Rebecca Campbell, Joe Coca, Jamie Hogsett, Kerry Jackson, Katrina Loving, Pamela Norman, Ann Swanson, and Tricia Waddell. And also to the wonderful artisans and manufacturers who made such beautiful products for us to work with.

Most importantly, thank you to the readers of this book who find metal beads, chain, and findings—gold to gunmetal, bronze to brass—as irresistible as we do.

danielle & melinda

contents

introduction

think about it.

Just about every piece of jewelry you come across these days has at least some metallic element. Yet metal always seems to play a supporting role in books dedicated to jewelry making. Pearls, stones, charms—they're the ones that get all the good parts. With this book, however, we plan to change things!

What makes us think we're capable of giving metals their just desserts? First, as editors of *Beadwork* and *Stringing* magazines, we are exposed to some of the best metal beading materials on the market today. We're excited to share our knowledge of these beads and findings as well as all that we have learned about great design, proper beading and wireworking techniques, bead shopping, and, of course, having fun while making jewelry. Second, we've discovered that we're kindred bead-dork souls (in fact, we've confessed to each other that we have "inspiration insomnia"—a condition where you design projects in your sleep). In league together, we decided we might just be able to infect all who read this book with a love for beading, especially with metal beads and findings.

Our book is divided into five chapters, each of which discusses a type of metallic bead: gold, silver, base metals, faux and other metals, and mixing metals. Each opens with some background information on the featured metal(s), followed by four to five projects that show you how to combine the aforementioned metals with fabulous beads and findings. Many of the designs also have matching accessories, helping you create jewelry pieces that are sure to complement each other (and you).

Come across a term that you are unfamiliar with? Flip to the Glossary of Terms on p. 88. Looking for great places to shop for beads (isn't that half the fun anyway)? See pp. 105–108 for a detailed resource guide to the projects along with contact information for the featured bead artists and suppliers. Always wondered how to give your metal jewelry that great aged, artsy look? Page 101 tells you how to oxidize and color your metals.

We hope you find inspiration in each of our projects, whether you choose to replicate the projects exactly or use the designs as a springboard for your own creations (perhaps you'll fall in love with a design's color palette, the use of symmetry/asymmetry, or a combination of metals). Like us, you just may find yourself lying awake at night, dreaming up new ways to add a warm splash of gold or the cool touch of silver to your latest beading creation—we're sorry to tell you, there is no antidote.

gold

Since ancient times, gold has been considered the king of all metals. Warm, yellow, and shiny, its physical characteristics resemble those of the sun. This coincidence was not lost on ancient sun-worshipping civilizations that attributed divine characteristics to the metal. Archaeological evidence proves that by 4000 B.C., gold was highly valued and used in items of personal adornment.

Humans' reverence for gold is well-founded. Besides being pretty, gold can last forever—it does not rust, it does not tarnish, and it isn't corroded by the usual suspects: air, water, or common acids. It is the most malleable and ductile of the metals (an ounce of gold can be beaten into a 300-square-foot sheet or drawn into a wire more than fifty miles long!). Gold also readily forms alloys with other metals—an important quality, as pure gold is too soft to be usable.

Most often, it is alloyed with copper, silver, palladium, nickel, and/or iron for additional strength and to alter its color.

The karat system was developed to distinguish how much pure gold exists in a gold alloy. The word karat (or carat) comes from the Arabic word for bean seed, specifically the carob seed, which was used in ancient times to measure the weight of gold. Even today, pure or fine gold is designated as 24k gold, whereas 14k gold is 14 parts gold by weight and 10 parts of another metal or metals (or 58.5 percent pure). In the United States, an item must be at least 10k gold to be sold as gold.

Gold is found all over the world, but top producers are Australia, China, Peru, Russia, South Africa, and the United States. About two-thirds of all gold produced is used in jewelry.

rosy posies

for complete NECKLACE instructions
PAGE
14

PAGE **16**

for complete NECKLACE & BRACELET instructions

greta
garbo

for complete NECKLACE & EARRING instructions

PAGE
18

first lady

golden
blush

for complete NECKLACE & EARRING instructions

PAGE
20

{rosy posies}

Wrap flower-tipped rose-gold head pins around a vermeil ring to create a wreathlike pendant that sings the praises of pink!

materials

1 vermeil 55mm hammered ring

1 rose-gold vermeil 60mm decorative head pin with 11×6mm flower

2 rose-gold vermeil 62mm decorative head pins with 15×5mm flowers

2 rose-gold vermeil 65mm decorative head pins with 9mm tulips

2 rose-gold vermeil 72mm decorative head pins with 10×5mm flowers

1 vermeil 70mm decorative head pin with 9×18mm leaf

1 rose-gold vermeil 10×20mm flower S-clasp with 2 attached 6mm soldered jump rings

3 rose-gold vermeil 6mm jump rings

24½" (62 cm) of rose-gold vermeil 5mm round chain

3' (91.5 cm) of rose-gold vermeil 26-gauge wire

TOOLS

2 pairs of chain- or flat-nose pliers; wire cutters

FINISHED SIZE
25½" (65 cm)

TECHNIQUES USED
(see how-to, pp. 97–103)
Jump rings; stringing

VERMEIL
(pronounced *vehr-may*) beads and findings have a sterling (or fine) silver base that is bonded with a layer of gold, which must be at least 10k gold.

ROSE- (OR PINK-) GOLD VERMEIL beads and findings have a different appearance than regular vermeil. They have a sterling (or fine) silver base that is bonded with a layer of rose gold, a gold alloy that contains a relatively high percentage of copper (thus the reddish tint) and usually some silver.

1 Hold the flower end of one 72mm head pin snugly on top of one side of the vermeil ring (this will hereafter be referred to as the front of the ring). Tightly wrap the tail of the head pin twice around the ring, being careful not to push against the back of the flower in a way that will break the flower off the pin (the soldered joint can be fragile). Trim the tail of the head pin at the back of the ring.

2 Repeat Step 1 seven times to attach the remaining head pins to one half of the ring, placing each about ⅛ to ⅜" (3 mm to 1 cm) apart, with the leaf in the center.

3 Use chain-nose pliers to make a 90° bend ⅛" (3 mm) from one end of the 26-gauge wire. Hold the bent ⅛" of wire flat against the back of the ring, parallel to the back of the ring, and about ¼" (6 mm) away from the row of head pins, making sure the end of the bent wire points toward the first flower added. Tightly wrap the working end of the wire several times around the ring to cover the ⅛" (3 mm) tail, placing the wraps snugly next to each other and working your way toward the first flower.

4 When you reach the first flower, wrap as closely as possible up to one side of the flower, then begin wrapping again on the other side of the flower. You will need to wrap over the head-pin wraps.

5 Continue wrapping the wire around the ring and up to the last flower. Make wraps for another 1¼" (6 mm) beyond the last flower, stopping with the wire on the front side of the ring.

6 Use the wire to string the last link on one end of the piece of chain, then wrap once more around the ring while holding the chain link on the outside (edge) of the ring. Make 3 more wraps around the ring and through the chain link, securing the chain to the ring. To finish, make 3 perpendicular wraps between the chain link and the ring, then trim the wire at the back of the ring.

7 Use 1 jump ring to attach the free end of the chain to one of the clasp's soldered jump rings.

8 Attach 1 jump ring to the bare half of the vermeil ring. Use another jump ring to attach the previous jump ring to the clasp's free soldered jump ring.

{greta garbo}

Take two of jewelry's hottest components—crystals and gold findings—string them up into a necklace and matching bracelet, and, baby, you'll be screen-goddess glam!

materials

NECKLACE

10 jet 6×3mm crystal spacers

8 jet 8mm crystal rounds

8 jet crystal/gold-plated 5×2mm rondelles

10 jet crystal/gold-plated 6×3mm rondelles

10 jet crystal/gold-plated 8mm rhinestone rounds

11 jet crystal/gold-plated 10mm rhinestone rounds

1 jet crystal/gold-plated 15mm square filigree

1 gold-plated 7×12mm lobster clasp

1 gold-plated 3×4mm oval jump ring

2 gold-filled 2mm crimp tubes

2 gold-filled 3mm crimp covers

6" (15 cm) of jet crystal with gold-plated bezels 6×12mm round chain

15½" (39.5 cm) of gold satin .018 beading wire

BRACELET

2 jet 6×3mm crystal rondelles

2 jet crystal/gold-plated 5×2mm rondelles

1 jet crystal/gold-plated 10mm rhinestone round

1 gold-plated 7×12mm lobster clasp

1 jet crystal/gold-plated 24-gauge 1½" (38mm) decorative head pin

2 gold-filled 2mm crimp tubes

2 gold-filled 3mm crimp covers

1¾" (4.5 cm) of gold-plated 5×7mm textured oval chain

5" (12.5 cm) of jet crystal with gold-plated bezels 6×12mm round chain

3½" (9 cm) of gold satin .018 beading wire

TOOLS

Crimping pliers; 2 pairs of chain- or flat-nose pliers; round-nose pliers; wire cutters

FINISHED SIZE

Necklace: 19" (48.5 cm)

Bracelet: 6¾" (17 cm), adjustable to 8½" (21.5 cm)

TECHNIQUES USED

(see how-to, pp. 97–103)

Crimping; jump rings; stringing; wrapped loop

GOLD-PLATED beads and findings are bonded with a layer of gold that must be at least 10k—the same requirement as gold-filled. The difference is that the layer need not be ¹⁄₂₀ of the piece's weight; it can be much thinner.

tip *The crystal chain is formed by jump rings connecting crystal-bezel links. When you purchase this chain, or when you take it apart to form different segments, you may lose jump rings on some of the links; therefore, you will want to purchase a couple extra matching 3×4mm oval jump rings just in case.*

necklace

1 Attach 1 jump ring to one side of the filigree. Attach the jump ring on one end of one 3" (7.5 cm) piece (5 links) of crystal chain to the other side of the filigree.

2 Use the beading wire to string 1 crimp tube and the free end of the previous chain; pass back through the tube and crimp. Cover the tube with 1 crimp cover. String {1 jet round and one 5×2mm rondelle} four times. String {one 8mm rhinestone round and 1 jet spacer} five times. String {one 10mm rhinestone round and one 6×3mm rondelle} ten times. String one 10mm rhinestone round. String {1 jet spacer and one 8mm rhinestone round} five times. String {one 5×2mm rondelle and 1 jet round} four times. String 1 crimp tube and one end of one 3" (7.5 cm) piece (5 links) of crystal chain; pass back through the tube, crimp, and cover.

3 Attach the jump ring on the free end of the previous chain to the clasp.

4 To wear, attach the clasp to the first jump ring attached to the filigree in Step 1.

bracelet

1 Attach the jump ring on one end of one ¾" (2 cm) piece (1 link) of crystal chain to the clasp.

2 Use the beading wire to string 1 crimp tube and the free end of the previous chain link; pass back through the tube and crimp. Cover the tube with 1 crimp cover. Use the beading wire to string one 6×3mm rondelle, one 5×2mm rondelle, the rhinestone round, one 5×2mm rondelle, one 6×3mm rondelle, 1 crimp tube, and one end of one 4⅝" (11.8 cm) piece (8 links) of crystal chain. Pass back through the crimp tube; crimp and cover.

3 Attach the jump ring on the free end of the previous chain to one end of the oval chain. Use the head pin to form a wrapped loop that attaches to the other end of the oval chain.

{first lady}

Jewel tones look fabulous paired with gold. Here, this classic color combination is carried out in a necklace and earring set made with navy pearls and gold-plated beads and findings.

materials

NECKLACE
4 night blue 3mm crystal pearls
14 night blue 4mm crystal pearls
37 night blue 5mm crystal pearls
64 night blue 6mm crystal pearls
17 night blue 8mm crystal pearls
6 gold-plated 7×5mm button beads
12 gold-plated 10mm rose rounds
14 gold-plated 10mm floral coins
1 gold-plated 12mm rose box clasp
7" (18 cm) of navy blue 7mm synthetic satin ribbon
2 gold-filled 2mm crimp tubes
2 gold-filled 3mm crimp covers
49" (124.5 cm) of gold satin .018 beading wire

EARRINGS
2 night blue 6mm crystal pearls
2 gold-plated 20mm floral pendants with off-center openings
2 gold-plated 2" (50mm) head pins
1 pair of vermeil ear wires

TOOLS
2 bead stops; crimping pliers; lighter or match; scissors; wire cutters

FINISHED SIZE
Necklace
Shortest strand: 21" (53.5 cm)
Longest strand: 23" (58.5 cm)
Earrings (including ear wires): 1½" (3.8 cm)

TECHNIQUES USED
(see how-to, pp. 97–103)
Crimping; stringing; wrapped loop

GOLD-PLATED GERMAN METAL beads have a tin base (findings have a brass base) that is bonded with a layer of 22k gold. The pieces are then given a matte finish and treated with a lacquer coating.

necklace

1 Attach 1 bead stop to one end of one 25½" (65 cm) piece of beading wire. String one 3mm pearl. String {1 gold round and one 5mm pearl} twelve times. String 3 button beads. String nine 8mm pearls. String thirty-three 6mm pearls. String sixteen 5mm pearls. String one 3mm pearl. Attach the remaining bead stop to the end of the beading wire.

2 Secure one end of one 23½" (59.5 cm) piece of beading wire in the first bead stop used in Step 1 along with the first strand. String one 3mm pearl. String {1 gold coin and one 4mm pearl} fourteen times. String 3 button beads. String eight 8mm pearls. String thirty-one 6mm pearls. String nine 5mm pearls. String one 3mm pearl. Secure the end of the beading wire in the second bead stop used in Step 1 along with the first strand.

3 Remove the first bead stop used in Step 1 and use both beading wires to string 1 crimp tube and the tab half of the clasp. Pass back through the tube and crimp. Cover the tube with 1 crimp cover.

4 Remove the second bead stop and use both beading wires to string 1 crimp tube and the box half of the clasp. Snug the beads, pass back through the tube, and crimp. Cover the tube with 1 crimp cover.

5 Use the ribbon to tie a bow that covers the previous crimp cover. Trim the ends of the ribbon at an angle. Use the lighter or match to slightly melt the very ends of the ribbon to prevent fraying.

earrings

1 Use 1 head pin to string 1 pearl and 1 pendant, passing through the pendant from the inside out; form a wrapped loop that attaches to 1 ear wire.

2 Repeat Step 1 for a second earring.

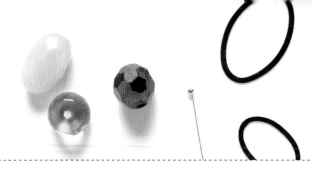

{golden blush}

The warm tones of gold-filled components perfectly complement the soft natural beads used in this long, organic necklace. For a shorter necklace, wrap it around your neck twice.

materials

NECKLACE

- 3 metallic bronze 10mm faceted glass rounds
- 3 pink 11×7mm faceted quartz rondelles
- 4 white howlite 12mm rounds
- 3 peach moonstone 10×13–15mm faceted ovals
- 3 natural 18×35mm mother-of-pearl rectangles
- 3 natural-and-black 15mm flower-print bone coins
- 3 natural-and-brown 18mm assorted bone flowers
- 2 dark brown 12mm filigree wood rounds
- 2 light brown 15mm filigree wood rounds
- 2 gold-filled 13×20mm (small) flat oval rings
- 1 gold-filled 18×28mm (large) flat oval ring
- 1 gold-filled 6×12mm lobster clasp
- 1 gold-filled 4mm jump ring
- 11" (28 cm) of gold-filled 2×3mm flat oval chain
- 8" (20.5 cm) of gold-filled 6×8mm flat oval chain
- 6' (183 cm) of gold-filled 24-gauge half-hard wire

EARRINGS

- 2 natural 10×12mm mother-of-pearl rectangles
- 2 gold-filled 24-gauge 2" (50mm) ball-end head pins
- 1 pair of gold-filled 18×43mm ear wires
- 5" (12.5 cm) of gold-filled 2×3mm flat oval chain

TOOLS

Chain-nose pliers; round-nose pliers; wire cutters

FINISHED SIZE

Necklace: 34" (86.5 cm)
Earrings (including ear wires): 2" (5 cm)

TECHNIQUES USED

(see how-to, pp. 97–103)
Jump rings; stringing; wrapped loop

> **GOLD-FILLED** beads and findings are made of a base metal that is bonded with a layer of gold, which must be at least 10k gold and equal to at least $1/20$ of the whole piece's weight.

necklace

1 Use 4" (10 cm) of wire to form a wrapped loop. Use the end of the wire to string one end of two 1¾" (4.5 cm) pieces of 2×3mm chain. String 1 mother-of-pearl rectangle. Bring 1 of the pieces of chain up one side of the rectangle and use the wire to string the free end of the chain, removing links from the end, if necessary, so that the chain lies snugly against the side of the rectangle; repeat with the other piece of chain, laying it against the other side of the rectangle. Form a wrapped loop to create a link. Repeat entire step twice for a total of 3 mother-of-pearl links. Set aside.

2 Cut the 6×8mm chain into four 1⅞" (4.7 cm) pieces. Use the jump ring to attach the lobster clasp to one end of 1 piece of 6×8mm chain. Use 2½" (6.5 cm) of wire to form a wrapped loop that attaches to the other end of the previous chain. String 1 pink quartz; form a wrapped loop.

3 Use 2½" (6.5 cm) of wire to form a wrapped loop that attaches to the previous wrapped loop. String 1 metallic bronze round; form a wrapped loop. Use 2½" (6.5 cm) of wire to form a wrapped loop that attaches to the previous wrapped loop. String 1 white howlite; form a wrapped loop. Use 2½" (6.5 cm) of wire to form a wrapped loop that attaches to the previous wrapped loop. String one 15mm wood round; form a wrapped loop that attaches to one end of 1 mother-of-pearl link.

4 Use 2½" (6.5 cm) of wire to form a wrapped loop that attaches to the other end of the previous mother-of-pearl link. String 1 peach moonstone; form a wrapped loop that attaches to one end of 1 piece of 6×8mm chain. Use 3" (7.5 cm) of wire to form a wrapped loop that attaches to the other end of the previous chain. String 1 bone flower; form a wrapped loop. Use 2½" (6.5 cm) of wire to form a wrapped loop that attaches to the previous wrapped loop. String 1 bone coin; form a wrapped loop that attaches to one end of 1 mother-of-pearl link.

5 Use 2½" (6.5 cm) of wire to form a wrapped loop that attaches to the other end of the previous mother-of-pearl link. String 1 pink quartz; form a wrapped loop that attaches to one end of the large flat oval ring.

6 Use 2½" (6.5 cm) of wire to form a wrapped loop that attaches to the other end of the large flat oval ring. String 1 white howlite; form a wrapped loop. Use 2½" (6.5 cm) of wire to form a wrapped loop that attaches to the previous wrapped loop. String one 12mm wood round; form a wrapped loop. Use 2½" (6.5 cm) of wire to form a wrapped loop that attaches to the previous wrapped loop. String 1 bone coin; form a wrapped loop. Use 2½" (6.5 cm) of wire to form a wrapped loop that attaches to the previous wrapped loop. String 1 metallic bronze round; form a wrapped loop. Use 2½" (6.5 cm) of wire to form a wrapped loop that attaches to the previous wrapped loop. String 1 peach moonstone; form a wrapped loop that attaches to one end of 1 piece of 6×8mm chain.

7 Use 3" (7.5 cm) of wire to form a wrapped loop that attaches to the other end of the previous chain. String 1 bone flower; form a wrapped loop. Use 2½" (6.5 cm) of wire to form a wrapped loop that attaches to the previous wrapped loop.

String 1 white howlite; form a wrapped loop. Use 2½" (6.5 cm) of wire to form a wrapped loop that attaches to the previous wrapped loop. String one 15mm wood round; form a wrapped loop that attaches to one end of the remaining mother-of-pearl link.

8 Use 2½" (6.5 cm) of wire to form a wrapped loop that attaches to the other end of the previous mother-of-pearl link. String 1 pink quartz; form a wrapped loop. Use 3" (7.5 cm) of wire to form a wrapped loop that attaches to the previous wrapped loop. String 1 bone flower; form a wrapped loop that attaches to one end of 1 small flat oval ring.

9 Use 2½" (6.5 cm) of wire to form a wrapped loop that attaches to the other end of the previous small flat oval ring. String 1 metallic bronze round; form a wrapped loop. Use 2½" (6.5 cm) of wire to form a wrapped loop that attaches to the previous wrapped loop. String 1 bone coin; form a wrapped loop that attaches to one end of the remaining piece of 6×8mm chain.

10 Use 2½" (6.5 cm) of wire to form a wrapped loop that attaches to the other end of the previous chain. String 1 white howlite; form a wrapped loop. Use 2½" (6.5 cm) of wire to form a wrapped loop that attaches to the previous wrapped loop. String 1 peach moonstone; form a wrapped loop. Use 2½" (6.5 cm) of wire to form a wrapped loop that attaches to the previous wrapped loop. String one 12mm wood round; form a wrapped loop that attaches to one end of the remaining small flat oval ring.

To wear, attach the lobster clasp to the other end of the previous ring.

earrings

1 Use 1 head pin to string one end of two 1" (2.5 cm) pieces of 2×3mm chain. String 1 mother-of-pearl rectangle. Bring 1 of the pieces of chain up one side of the rectangle and use the wire to string the free end of the chain, removing links from the end, if necessary, so that the chain lies snugly against the side of the rectangle; repeat with the other piece of chain, laying it against the other side of the rectangle. Form a wrapped loop that attaches to the loop of 1 ear wire.

2 Repeat Step 1 for a second earring.

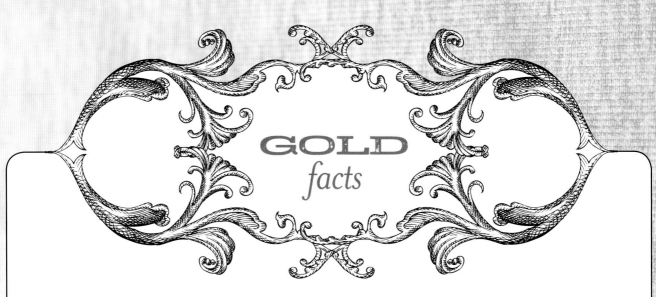

GOLD
facts

✦ The chemical symbol for gold, Au, is an abbreviation of the Latin word for gold, aurum, which means "shining dawn."

✦ Though gold is often considered the most precious of the precious metals, platinum is actually more valuable. At the time of press, platinum was trading at two times the price of gold.

✦ Nevada is the top gold-producing state in the United States.

✦ Want to know your weight in gold? Visit www.onlygold.com.

✦ King Tutankhamen (a famous Egyptian Pharaoh who died about 1400 B.C.) was buried in an inner coffin made of solid gold.

✦ The word gold has many positive associations: To have a heart of gold means to be very kind. To be as good as gold is to be of the highest worth. The golden rule is an important principle, usually to do unto others as you would have them do unto you.

✦ It is estimated that 90 percent of the world's gold has been produced since 1848, the year of California's famous gold rush.

✦ "I love gooold"—a quote from the villain Goldmember in the Austin Powers movie of the same name.

✦ Gold is found all over the world but rarely in quantities large enough to be deemed worth extracting.

✦ Metaphysicists dub gold the "master healer" and attribute to the metal the power of relieving stress and anger, attracting positive energy, and balancing energies.

✦ Gold has long been used by glass-makers to tint glass a rich red color.

✦ It is estimated that about 15 percent of the gold in circulation is recycled. That means it is possible your gold-filled earrings were made with gold that was once part of an Egyptian Pharaoh's ensemble!

✦ Gold is considered a superb dental material as it is soft, durable, and nontoxic. Today, many hip-hop artists wear "grills," or gold caps, over their teeth as a sort of mouth jewelry.

English: *Gold* ✦ **French:** *Or* ✦ **German:** *das Gold*
Italian: *Oro* ✦ **Spanish:** *Oro* ✦ **Latin:** *Aurum*

silver

though silver is the most plentiful and inexpensive of the precious metals, it is second only to gold in its historic importance and, in pre-Christian times, may even have surpassed gold in popularity. As gold's warm hue was often associated with the sun, so silver's cool, white luster was associated with the moon. Evidence of the metal being mined dates back to around 4000 B.C., and it is known that silver was prized by ancient civilizations in North and South America, Greece, Spain, Rome, and China.

Despite being the antithesis of gold in appearance and about half its weight, silver actually has properties similar to gold: It, too, is very malleable and ductile (though slightly less so than gold), and in its pure state, it must be alloyed with another metal (usually copper) to be rendered usable. Like gold, silver is stable in pure air and water, but, unlike gold, it tarnishes in the presence of sulfur compounds. Interestingly, tarnish wasn't much of an issue before the Industrial Revolution, when factories started polluting the air and water.

The standard for determining the fineness or purity of silver was established in early medieval England. The combination of 925 parts silver to 75 parts copper (a perfect balance of silver purity and sufficient hardness for durability) was declared the silver standard, also known as sterling silver. Today, items sold as sterling silver must be marked as "925."

From about 1500 to 1800, the New World (specifically Central and South America) was the source of most silver, though the discovery of the Comstock Lode in Nevada in 1859 and other American sources distinguished the United States as the top silver producer until the 1900s. Today, the top silver producers are Australia, Chile, China, Mexico, and Peru. An estimated 20 percent of all silver produced is used in jewelry applications.

for complete NECKLACE instructions

PAGE
30

ghost
ranch

silver shade

for complete NECKLACE & BRACELET instructions

PAGE
32

silver
lining

for complete NECKLACE instructions

PAGE
36

PAGE 38

for complete BRACELET & EARRING instructions

silvered
buds

{ghost ranch}

Artisan-made fine silver chain, fine silver-accented beach-glass beads, and a lampworked pendant—yes, the "tusk" pendant is glass!—are rounded up in a necklace that Georgia O'Keeffe might have worn on her New Mexico ranch.

materials

- 1 green 9×20mm beach-glass nugget with fine silver bail
- 1 aqua 18×8mm beach-glass rondelle with fine silver caps
- 1 dark green 18×8mm beach-glass rondelle with fine silver caps
- 3 aquamarine 5×3mm faceted rondelles
- 1 fine silver 5×11mm bumpy tube
- 1 fine silver 12mm stamped ring
- 3 fine silver 4×17mm irregular stick charms
- 2 fine silver 10mm stamped round charms
- 2 fine silver 7×12mm stamped oval links
- 1 Thai silver 14mm round charm
- 1 cream-and-brown 12×52mm lamp-worked glass tusk-shaped pendant with fine silver bail
- 1 sterling silver 16mm hammered toggle clasp
- 14 sterling silver 6mm jump rings
- ¾" (2 cm) of Thai silver 8mm patterned round chain with unsoldered links
- 14½" (37 cm) of Thai silver 8mm hammered round chain
- 2⅞" (7.2 cm) of fine silver 12–15mm printed irregular-round chain
- 10½" (26.5 cm) of sterling silver 24-gauge wire
- Oxidizing materials (p. 101)

TOOLS
Chain-nose pliers; round-nose pliers; wire cutters

FINISHED SIZE
23¾" (60.5 cm)

TECHNIQUES USED
(see how-to, pp. 97–103)
Jump rings; oxidizing metal; wrapped loop

FINE SILVER beads and findings contain 99.9 percent pure silver. Crafters can make their own fine silver beads with Precious Metal Clay (PMC), a substance that, when heated at a high temperature, releases stabilizers and leaves behind only pure silver.

of the previous stamped oval link to one end of one 3⅞" (9.7 cm) piece of hammered chain.

5 Use 1 jump ring to attach 1 stick charm to the sixth chain link from the stamped oval link; repeat twice to attach stick charms to the eighth and tenth chain links. Use 1 jump ring to attach one 10mm round charm to the seventh link; repeat, attaching the remaining charm to the ninth chain link. Use 1 jump ring to attach the 14mm round charm to the twelfth chain link. Use the end of the previous chain to string the pendant. Use 1 jump ring to attach the nugget to the fifteenth chain link. Use 1 jump ring to attach the free end of the previous chain to one end of the fine silver chain.

6 Repeat Step 3, using the aqua rondelle and attaching the first bail to the free end of the fine silver chain and the second bail to one end of one 3⅝" (9 cm) piece of hammered chain.

7 Use 1 jump ring to attach one end of 1 stamped oval link to the free end of the previous chain. Use 2½" (6.5 cm) of wire to form a wrapped loop that attaches to the other end of the previous stamped oval link. String 1 aquamarine rondelle, the bumpy tube, and 2 aquamarine rondelles; form a wrapped loop that attaches to one end of the patterned chain. Open the link at the other end of the previous chain as you would a jump ring; string the stamped ring and close the link.

8 Use 1 jump ring to attach the previous ring to one end of one 2⅝" (6.5 cm) piece of hammered chain. Use 1 jump ring to attach the free end of the previous chain to the bar half of the clasp.

necklace

1 Oxidize the wire, jump rings, and all chains, except the fine silver chain.

2 Use 1 jump ring to attach 1 link of hammered chain to the ring half of the clasp.

3 Use 2" (5 cm) of wire and the dark green rondelle to form a wrapped-loop bail that attaches to the previous chain link. Use 2" (5 cm) of wire and the other side of the dark green rondelle to form a wrapped-loop bail that attaches to one end of one 3⅝" (9 cm) piece of hammered chain.

4 Use 1 jump ring to attach one end of 1 stamped oval link to the free end of the previous chain. Use 1 jump ring to attach the other end

{silver shade}

Matte fine silver- and oxidized fine silver-plated beads and findings harmonize beautifully in this metal-rich necklace and bracelet ensemble.

materials

NECKLACE

14 clear 8mm quartz rounds

23 fine silver-plated 6mm lentils

2 fine silver-plated 7mm rounds

2 oxidized fine silver-plated 6mm trumpet flowers

16 oxidized fine silver-plated 9×3mm flat flowers

2 oxidized fine silver-plated 11×26mm willow-leaf pendants

1 oxidized fine silver-plated 12mm rose box clasp

15 fine silver-plated 4mm jump rings

8 fine silver-plated 6mm jump rings

12 oxidized fine silver-plated 6mm jump rings

6 oxidized fine silver-plated 24-gauge 2" (50mm) head pins

5 oxidized fine silver-plated 24-gauge 4¾" (120mm) head pins *or* 21" (53.5 cm) of oxidized sterling silver 24-gauge wire

2 sterling silver 2mm crimp tubes

2 sterling silver 3mm crimp covers

11" (28 cm) of fine silver–plated 5×8mm oval chain

3" (7.5 cm) of black .021 beading wire

BRACELET

7 clear 8mm quartz rounds

5 fine silver-plated 7mm rounds

4 oxidized fine silver–plated 6mm trumpet flowers

4 oxidized fine silver–plated 9×3mm flat flowers

5 oxidized fine silver–plated 8×15mm rondelles

3 oxidized fine silver–plated 11×26mm willow-leaf pendants

1 fine silver-plated 7×12mm lobster clasp

1 fine silver-plated 24-gauge 2" (50mm) head pin

8 oxidized fine silver–plated 24-gauge 2" (50mm) head pins

3 oxidized fine silver–plated 24-gauge 4¾" (120mm) head pins *or* 10½" (26.5 cm) of oxidized sterling silver 24-gauge wire

2 sterling silver 2mm crimp tubes

2 sterling silver 3mm crimp covers

2¼" (5.5 cm) of fine silver-plated 5×8mm oval chain

5½" (14 cm) of black .021 beading wire

TOOLS

Crimping pliers; 2 pairs of chain- or flat-nose pliers; round-nose pliers; wire cutters

FINISHED SIZE

Necklace: 19½" (49.5 cm)

Bracelet: 7" (18 cm), adjustable to 9" (23 cm)

TECHNIQUES USED

(see how-to, pp. 97–103)

Crimping; jump rings; simple loop; stringing; wrapped loop

SILVER-PLATED beads and findings are made of a base metal coated with a thin layer of fine silver. Silver-colored beads categorized as German metal have a tin base (findings have a brass base) bonded with fine silver and a matte finish treated with a lacquer coating.

---

necklace

1 Cut the 4¾" (120mm) head pins into fourteen 1½" (3.8 cm) pieces of oxidized wire, discarding the heads; set aside.

2 Use 1 oxidized jump ring to attach 1 flat flower and 1 pendant to one end of one 7" (18 cm) piece (34 links) of chain (this will hereafter be referred to as Link 1 of this piece of chain; the link at the other end of this piece of chain will be referred to as Link 34); repeat to attach another flat flower and pendant to Link 3. Use 1 oxidized jump ring to attach 1 flat flower to Links 2, 4, and 5. Use one 2" (50mm) head pin to string 1 flat flower; form a wrapped loop that attaches to Link 4. Use 1 fine silver 6mm jump ring to attach 1 lentil to Links 2, 3, 5, and 6. Use 1 fine silver 4mm jump ring to attach 1 lentil to Links 32, 33, and 34; repeat to attach a second lentil to Link 34.

3 Use 1 fine silver 4mm jump ring to attach the free end (Link 34) of the previous chain to the tab half of the clasp. Use 1 fine silver 4mm jump ring to attach 1 lentil to the previous 4mm jump ring; use 1 oxidized jump ring to attach 1 flat flower to the same jump ring. Set aside.

4 Use one 2" (50mm) head pin to string 1 trumpet flower; form a wrapped loop. Attach 1 fine silver 4mm jump ring to 1 lentil; repeat twice for a total of 3 lentil dangles. *Use one 2" (50mm) head pin to string 1 flat flower; form a wrapped loop. Repeat from * twice for a total of 3 flat-flower dangles. Use one 1½" (3.8 cm) piece of oxidized wire (cut in Step 1) to form a simple loop; string 1 quartz and form a simple loop.

5 Use the beading wire to string 1 crimp tube and the box half of the clasp; pass back through the tube and crimp. Cover the tube with 1 crimp cover. String 1 lentil dangle, 2 flat-flower

dangles (these dangles and the following dangles and link were formed in Step 4), 1 silver round, 1 flat-flower dangle, 1 lentil dangle, 1 trumpet-flower dangle, 1 lentil dangle, 1 silver round, 1 crimp tube, and one end of the quartz link. Pass back through the tube; crimp and cover.

6 Use one 1½" (3.8 cm) piece of oxidized wire to form a simple loop that attaches to the free end of the previous quartz link; string 1 quartz and form a simple loop. Repeat eleven times for a chain of 13 links.

7 Use one 2" (50mm) head pin to string 1 trumpet flower; form a wrapped loop. Attach 1 fine silver 4mm jump ring to 1 lentil; repeat for a second lentil dangle.

8 Open the last simple loop formed in Step 6 as you would a jump ring and string the 3 dangles from Step 7 and one end of one 3½" (9 cm) piece (17 links) of chain (this will hereafter be referred to as Link 1 on this piece of chain); close the loop. Use 1 fine silver 4mm jump ring to attach 1 lentil to Links 1, 2, 3, and 4; repeat to attach a second lentil dangle to Link 3. Use 1 fine silver 6mm jump ring to attach 1 lentil to Links 14, 16, and 17. Use 1 oxidized 6mm jump ring to attach 1 flat flower to Links 2, 15, 16, and 17; repeat to attach a second flat flower to Link 17.

9 Use one 1½" (3.8 cm) piece of oxidized wire to form a simple loop that attaches to the free end (Link 17) of the chain used in Step 8; string 1 quartz and form a simple loop that attaches to Link 5 of the chain used in Steps 2 and 3 (this completes the Y shape of the necklace). Use 1 fine silver 6mm jump ring to attach 1 lentil to the second simple loop just formed; repeat using 1 oxidized jump ring and 1 flat flower.

bracelet

1 Cut the 4¾" (120mm) head pins into seven 1½" (3.8 cm) pieces of oxidized wire, discarding the heads; set aside.

2 Use the fine silver head pin to string 1 silver round; form a wrapped loop that attaches to one end of the chain.

3 Use one 1½" (3.8 cm) piece of oxidized wire to form a simple loop that attaches to the free end of the previous chain; string 1 quartz and form a simple loop. *Use one 1½" (3.8 cm) piece of oxidized wire to form a simple loop that attaches to the previous simple loop; string 1 quartz and form a simple loop. Repeat from * five times for a chain of 7 links.

4 Use 1 oxidized head pin to string 1 flat flower; form a wrapped loop. Use 1 oxidized head pin to string 1 trumpet flower and form a wrapped loop; repeat for a second trumpet-flower dangle. Use 1 oxidized head pin to string 1 flat flower and 1 pendant; form a wrapped loop.

5 Open the last simple loop formed in Step 3 as you would a jump ring and string 1 trumpet-flower dangle (this and the following dangles were formed in Step 4), the flat-flower/pendant dangle, the flat-flower dangle, and the remaining trumpet-flower dangle; close the loop.

6 Use 1 oxidized head pin to string 1 trumpet flower and form a wrapped loop; repeat for a second trumpet-flower dangle. Use 1 oxidized head pin to string 1 flat flower and 1 pendant; form a wrapped loop and repeat for a second flat-flower/pendant dangle.

7 Use the beading wire to string 1 crimp tube and the last simple loop formed in Step 3, between the flat-flower/pendant dangle and the flat-flower dangle; pass back through the tube and crimp. Cover the tube with 1 crimp cover. String {1 oxidized rondelle and 1 silver round} four times. String {1 trumpet-flower dangle (this and the following dangles were formed in Step 6) and 1 flat-flower/pendant dangle} twice. String 1 oxidized rondelle, 1 crimp tube, and the lobster clasp. Pass back through the tube; crimp and cover.

SILVER
facts

✦ In ancient times, slaves were used to extract silver from lead, since it was common for silver miners to die from lead poisoning.

✦ Silver has long been associated with magic, mystery, and romance. For example, Count Dracula could only be killed with a silver bullet or a stake through his heart.

✦ Metaphysically speaking, silver is believed to deliver patience and perseverance and helps channel the energies of gemstones.

✦ Paul Revere is one of America's most famous silversmiths.

✦ It was long ago discovered that silver has purification, antibacterial, and other healthful qualities. The expression "born with a silver spoon in one's mouth" not only means born into wealth, but also born into health, since it was noted in the 1800s that babies fed with silver spoons were healthier than those fed with other types of spoons.

✦ Silver has the most reflectivity of all the metals—when polished to a shine, it can be almost 100 percent reflective; hence it was often used for mirrors.

✦ Silver conducts electricity better than any other metal.

✦ Silver is the whitest of all the metals.

✦ Silver is often plated with rhodium to prevent tarnish.

✦ One theory states that the word "sterling" in association with silver dates back to the seventeenth century when a group of Germans known as Easterlings became renowned in Europe for the uniform quality of their silver coins, which were dubbed Easterlings, later shortened to sterlings.

English: *Silver* ✦ **French:** *Argent* ✦ **German:** *Silber*
Italian: *Argento* ✦ **Latin:** *Argentum* ✦ **Spanish:** *Plata*

{silver lining}

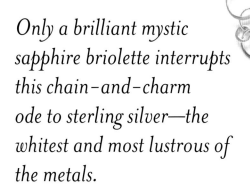

Only a brilliant mystic sapphire briolette interrupts this chain-and-charm ode to sterling silver—the whitest and most lustrous of the metals.

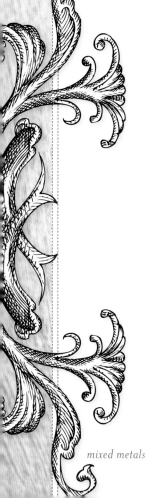

materials

1 mystic sapphire 8x14mm top-drilled faceted teardrop

1 sterling silver 6x8mm round charm with diamond and attached 4mm soldered jump ring

1 sterling silver 2x20mm teardrop charm

1 sterling silver 7x15mm "soar" tag charm with attached 5mm soldered jump ring

1 sterling silver 13x41mm openwork angel-wing pendant with attached 7mm soldered jump ring

1 sterling silver 21mm hammered ring

1 sterling silver 10x26mm hook-and-eye clasp

3 sterling silver 4mm jump rings

7 sterling silver 6mm jump rings

7¾" (19.5 cm) of sterling silver 3mm (small) flat round chain

10" (25.5 cm) of sterling silver 5/8/10mm (large) graduated flat round chain

10" (25.5 cm) of sterling silver 24-gauge wire

TOOLS
2 pairs of chain- or flat-nose pliers; round-nose pliers; wire cutters

FINISHED SIZE
18" (45.5 cm)

TECHNIQUES USED
(see how-to, pp. 97–103)
Jump rings; wrapped loop

STERLING SILVER beads and findings are made of a high-quality silver alloy that is required by law to have a content of 92.5 percent pure silver. All goods sold as sterling silver must have a "925" stamp.

mixed metals

tip *The "mystic" part of the material mystic sapphire refers to the coating applied to the sapphire.*

1 Use the wire and the mystic sapphire teardrop to form a wrapped-loop bail; do not trim the wire. Continue wrapping the tail wire around the top ¼" (6 mm) or so of the teardrop. Trim the wire close to the teardrop.

2 Use wire cutters to remove the soldered jump rings attached to the diamond and "soar" charms and the angel-wing pendant. *Use one 6mm jump ring to attach the "soar" charm to the hammered ring; repeat from * four times, attaching the angel-wing pendant, wrapped mystic sapphire teardrop, long teardrop charm, and diamond charm, in that order, to the hammered ring.

3 Use one 6mm jump ring to attach the eye half of the clasp to the hammered ring between the "soar" and diamond charms.

4 Use one 4mm jump ring to attach one end of one 6¼" (16 cm) piece of large round chain to the hook half of the clasp. Use one 4mm jump ring to attach the other end of the large round chain to one end of the small round chain. Use one 4mm jump ring to attach the other end of the small round chain to one end of one 2" (5 cm) piece of large round chain. Use one 6mm jump ring to attach the other end of the large round chain to the hammered ring, between the diamond charm and the eye half of the clasp.

{silvered buds}

Thai silver and pressed-glass flowers play peekaboo in the centers of the unique Thai silver puffed-square beads used in this bracelet and pair of earrings.

materials

BRACELET

13 maroon 9×6mm 5-petal pressed-glass flowers

28 Thai silver 3×2mm flower-print rondelles

1 Thai silver 20×5mm flower bead

8 Thai silver 20mm flower-print puffed squares with open centers

8 Thai silver 7×9mm rosebud charms

4 Thai silver 7×9mm bellflower charms

13 sterling silver 24-gauge 2" (50mm) ball-end head pins

2 sterling silver 2mm crimp tubes

2 sterling silver 3mm crimp covers

14" (35.5 cm) of .024 beading wire

EARRINGS

4 maroon 9×6mm 5-petal pressed-glass flowers

2 Thai silver 3×2mm flower-print rondelles

2 Thai silver 20mm flower-print puffed squares with open centers

1 Thai silver 7×9mm rosebud charm

1 Thai silver 7×9mm bellflower charm

1 pair of sterling silver 12×25mm ear wires

6 sterling silver 24-gauge 2" (50mm) ball-end head pins

TOOLS

Chain-nose pliers; crimping pliers; round-nose pliers; wire cutters

FINISHED SIZE

Bracelet: 8" (20.5 cm)

Earrings (including ear wires): 1¾" (4.5 cm)

TECHNIQUES USED

(see how-to, pp. 97–103)

Crimping; stringing; wrapped loop

THAI SILVER beads and findings are made of 95 to 99 percent pure silver and are created by the people of the Karen hill tribe in Thailand.

bracelet

1 Use 1 head pin to string 1 pressed-glass flower (wide end first); form a wrapped loop. Repeat eleven times, using all but one each of the pressed-glass flowers and head pins, for a total of 12 pressed-glass-flower dangles.

2 Use the remaining head pin to string the remaining pressed-glass flower (wide end first) and the Thai silver flower bead (wide end first); form a wrapped loop.

3 Use the beading wire to string 1 crimp tube and the previous wrapped loop. Pass back through the tube and crimp; cover the tube with 1 crimp cover.

4 String one side of 1 puffed square. Pass the wire up through the center of the square, then string 1 rosebud charm, 1 pressed-glass-flower dangle, and 1 bellflower charm. Pass the wire down through the center of the square and through the other side of the square. String 1 rondelle.

5 String one side of 1 puffed square. Pass the wire up through the center of the square, then string 1 pressed-glass-flower dangle, 1 rosebud charm, and 1 pressed-glass-flower dangle. Pass the wire down through the center of the square and through the other side of the square. String 1 rondelle.

6 Repeat Steps 4 and 5 three times, omitting the final rondelle. String 1 crimp tube and 21 rondelles (or enough to form a loop that fits around the Thai silver flower bead). Pass back through the tube, snug the beads, and crimp; cover the tube with 1 crimp cover.

earrings

1 Use 1 head pin to string 1 pressed-glass flower (wide end first); form a wrapped loop. Repeat three times for a total of 4 pressed-glass-flower dangles.

2 Use 1 head pin to string 1 rondelle and one side of 1 puffed square. Pass the head pin up through the center of the square, then string 1 pressed-glass-flower dangle, 1 rosebud charm, and 1 pressed-glass-flower dangle. Pass the head pin down through the center of the square and through the other side of the square; form a wrapped loop that attaches to the loop of 1 ear wire.

3 Repeat Step 2 for a second earring, using 1 bellflower in place of the rosebud charm.

base metals

in jewelry terms a base metal is defined as any metal other than a precious metal. Common base metals used in jewelry making include brass, bronze, copper, gunmetal, and pewter. Some base metals are used as is, while others are plated with precious metals. As the price of precious metals continues to increase, so does the popularity of base metals—an exciting development, as base metals can add rich color and character to jewelry.

COPPER is a chemical element and, thus, not an alloy of other base metals. Copper is important to the jewelry trade not only because of its own intrinsic reddish orange beauty, but also because it is the primary alloy responsible for making both pure gold and pure silver strong enough to be usable. Archaeological findings indicate that copper has been used by humans since 8000 B.C. or earlier, leading many scholars to believe it was the first metal known to man.

BRONZE, an alloy of copper and tin, became so important to mankind that an entire historical period, the "Bronze Age" (beginning about 3000 B.C.), was named after it—a time when man utilized bronze to make tools and weapons. While natural bronze isn't widely used in jewelry today, it lends its name to a color or finish—a metallic dark brown—that is more popular than ever.

GUNMETAL, a nearly black metal, is actually a type of bronze, being an alloy of copper, tin, and sometimes a small amount of zinc. As its name suggests, gunmetal was originally used to make guns. Gunmetal can refer to any metal treated to resemble gunmetal or, more generally, as a metal with a shiny, steely gray finish.

BRASS is an alloy of copper and zinc. Brass used in jewelry (the more yellowy brass) is usually 80 to 95 percent copper, the rest being zinc. Brass dates back to the late Bronze Age and was most certainly prized for its resemblance to gold.

PEWTER, an alloy of tin (mostly), copper, and antimony, is estimated to date back to the Bronze Age as well. From the Middle Ages through the eighteenth century, the metal was widely used in everything, from tableware to toys to jewelry because of the ease with which it can be worked. Many pewter products used to contain lead for malleability, but nowadays the use of lead (due to its toxicity) is restricted by state and federal laws.

for complete BRACELET & EARRING instructions

PAGE
47

blooms in brass

luck, love & copper

for complete NECKLACE & EARRING instructions

PAGE
50

bronze **beauty**

for complete BRACELET & EARRING instructions

PAGE
52

lyrical
lariat

for complete NECKLACE instructions

PAGE
54

for complete NECLKACE instructions

PAGE
56

we ♥
pewter

{ blooms in brass }

Brass rings, bead caps, and vines lend a vintage quality to this delicate floral bracelet and its matching earrings.

materials

BRACELET

6 pale blue 8mm glass rounds

2 jade 6mm rounds

3 rhodonite 6mm rounds

3 rhodonite 8mm faceted rounds

1 raw brass 33mm hammered ring

1 antique brass 30×40mm branch connector

5 natural brass 6×3mm scalloped bead caps

4 natural brass 9×5mm foliage bead caps

1 natural brass 5×30mm leaf toggle bar

1 natural brass 16×26mm leaf toggle ring

10 natural brass 22-gauge 2" (50mm) head pins

4 antique brass 4mm jump rings

4 natural brass 5mm jump rings

10" (25.5 cm) of gunmetal 22-gauge craft wire

EARRINGS

4 rhodonite 6mm rounds

2 rhodonite 8mm faceted rounds

4 raw brass 33mm hammered rings

2 natural brass 6×4mm scalloped bead caps

2 natural brass 6×3mm blossom bead caps

2 natural brass 9×5mm foliage bead caps

6 natural brass 2" (50mm) head pins

1 pair of antique brass lever-back ear wires

1½" (3.8 cm) of antique brass 4×6mm oval chain with unsoldered links

1" (2.5 cm) of natural brass 5×7mm etched oval chain with unsoldered links

G-S Hypo Cement

Masking tape

TOOLS

2 pairs of chain- or flat-nose pliers; round-nose pliers; wire cutters

FINISHED SIZE

Bracelet: 7" (18 cm)

Earrings (including ear wires): 2⅜" (6 cm)

TECHNIQUES USED

(see how-to, pp. 97–103)

Jump rings; simple loop; stringing; wrapped loop

BRASS beads and findings are composed of copper and zinc. The term raw brass usually describes jewelry components that have a goldlike appearance, whereas natural brass components have a darker, bronze-like finish. Brass labeled as "antique" is a shade somewhere in between.

bracelet

1 Use 1 head pin to string the toggle bar from front to back; form a double simple loop. Attach one 5mm jump ring to the double simple loop. Attach one 5mm jump ring to the previous jump ring; repeat once to form a chain of 3 jump rings.

2 Use 2" (5 cm) of wire to form a wrapped loop that attaches to the free end of the jump-ring chain. String 1 pale blue round and form a wrapped loop that attaches to the hammered ring.

3 Use one 5mm and two 4mm jump rings to attach the other side of the hammered ring to one end of the connector. Use 2" (5 cm) of wire to form a wrapped loop that attaches to the other end of the connector. String 1 pale blue round and form a wrapped loop to create a link.

4 Use 2" (5 cm) of wire to form a wrapped loop that attaches to the other end of the previous link. String 1 pale blue round and form a wrapped loop. Repeat entire step twice for a total of 4 links, attaching the final wrapped loop to the toggle ring.

5 Use 1 head pin to string 1 jade round and 1 scalloped bead cap; form a wrapped loop. Use one 4mm jump ring to attach the dangle to the wrapped loop that attaches to the toggle ring. Repeat entire step using 1 rhodonite 8mm round and 1 foliage bead cap.

6 Use 1 head pin to string 1 rhodonite 6mm round and 1 scalloped bead cap; form a wrapped loop that attaches to the second wrapped loop formed in Step 3.

7 Use 1 head pin to string 1 rhodonite 8mm round and 1 foliage bead cap; form a wrapped loop that attaches to the end of the connector nearest the toggle ring. Repeat entire step three times to attach the following dangles so that there are 2 dangles on each end of the connector: 1 jade round and 1 scalloped bead cap; 1 pale blue round and 1 foliage bead cap; 1 rhodonite 6mm round and 1 scalloped bead cap.

8 Use 1 head pin to string 1 rhodonite 8mm round and 1 foliage bead cap; form a wrapped loop that attaches to one side of the hammered ring.

9 Use 1 head pin to string 1 rhodonite 6mm round and 1 scalloped bead cap; form a wrapped loop that attaches to the second wrapped loop formed in Step 2.

earrings

1 Use 2 narrow pieces of masking tape to join 2 rings, with the hammered surfaces facing out. Dab a small amount of cement in several places inside the rings. Allow to dry.

2 Use 1 head pin to string 1 blossom bead cap and 1 rhodonite 6mm round; form a wrapped loop. Use 1 head pin to string 1 rhodonite

6mm round and 1 scalloped bead cap; form a wrapped loop. Use 1 head pin to string 1 rhodonite 8mm round and 1 foliage bead cap; form a wrapped loop.

3 Take apart all of the links of chain, opening and closing the links as you would jump rings. Use 1 antique brass link to string the 8mm rhodonite dangle and the blossom/6mm rhodonite dangle; close the link. Use 1 antique brass link to attach the previous link to the rings from Step 1 and the remaining dangle. Attach 1 natural brass link to the previous link. Use 1 antique brass link to attach the previous link to 1 ear wire.

4 Repeat Steps 1–3 for a second earring.

{luck, love & copper}

You're in luck if you love copper: it's fairly inexpensive, it's easy to find, and boy does it look great when paired with sterling silver!

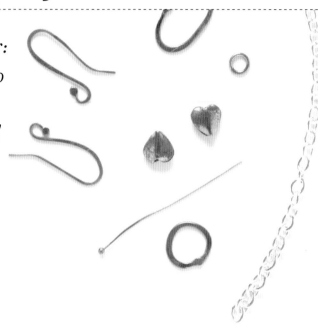

materials

NECKLACE

2 copper 8mm hearts with vertical holes

5 copper 8mm rounds

3 copper 10–12mm irregular-round rings

1 copper 12×20mm irregular-oval ring

1 sterling silver and copper 25×32mm horseshoe/flower pendant

1 sterling silver 6×11mm lobster clasp

6 sterling silver 5mm jump rings

12" (30.5 cm) of sterling silver 4×5mm oval chain

17½" (44.5 cm) of sterling silver 22-gauge wire

Oxidizing materials (p. 101)

EARRINGS

2 copper 8mm hearts with vertical holes

2 copper 12×20mm irregular-oval rings

1 pair of copper 12×25mm ear wires

2 copper 24-gauge 1½" (38mm) head pins

2" (5 cm) of sterling silver 4×5mm oval chain

Oxidizing materials (p. 101)

TOOLS

2 pairs of chain- or flat-nose pliers; round-nose pliers; wire cutters

FINISHED SIZE

Necklace: 17½" (44.5 cm)

Earrings (including ear wires): 2¼" (5.5 cm)

TECHNIQUES USED

(see how-to, pp. 97–103)

Jump rings; oxidizing metal; stringing; wrapped loop

COPPER is a metallic chemical element. Copper or copper-plated beads and findings can display colors from salmon red to brown to light bluish green.

necklace

1 Oxidize the copper rounds, lobster clasp, jump rings, and chain.

2 Use 2½" (6.5 cm) of wire to form a wrapped loop that attaches to 1 jump ring. String 1 heart (top to bottom) and form a wrapped loop that attaches to one end of one 3¼" (8.5 cm) piece of chain. Use 1 jump ring to attach the other end of the previous chain to 1 irregular-round ring.

3 Use 2½" (6.5 cm) of wire to form a wrapped loop that attaches to the previous irregular-round ring. String 1 copper round and form a wrapped loop that attaches to another irregular-round ring. Repeat entire step.

4 Use 1 jump ring to attach one end of one ½" (1.3 cm) piece of chain to the previous irregular-round ring. Use 2½" (6.5 cm) of wire to form a wrapped loop that attaches to the other end of the previous chain. String 1 heart (top to bottom) and form a wrapped loop that attaches to one end of one 1½" (3.8 cm) piece of chain. Use this chain to string the pendant, then use 1 jump ring to attach the free end of the chain to the irregular-oval ring.

5 Use 1 jump ring to attach one end of one ⅝" (1.5 cm) piece of chain to the irregular-oval ring. Use 2½" (6.5 cm) of wire to form a wrapped loop that attaches to the other end of the previous chain. String 1 copper round and form a wrapped loop.

6 Use 2½" (6.5 cm) of wire to form a wrapped loop that attaches to the previous wrapped loop. String 1 copper round and form a wrapped loop.

7 Use 2½" (6.5 cm) of wire to form a wrapped loop that attaches to the previous wrapped loop. String 1 copper round and form a wrapped loop that attaches to one end of one 3⅞" (9.7 cm) piece of chain. Use 1 jump ring to attach the other end of the chain to the lobster clasp. To wear, attach the lobster clasp to the jump ring used in Step 2.

earrings

1 Oxidize the chain.

2 Use 1 head pin to string 1 heart, bottom to top; form a wrapped loop that attaches to one end of one 1" (2.5 cm) piece of chain. Open the loop of 1 ear wire as you would a jump ring and use it to string 1 irregular-oval ring and the other end of the chain; close the ear-wire loop.

3 Repeat Step 2 for a second earring.

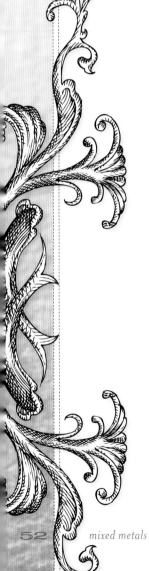

{bronze beauty}

A pure-bronze bracelet finding with a horse print is the showpiece of this cowgirl-chic bracelet and earring set. Hi ho, Bronze—away!

materials

BRACELET

162 matte fool's gold size 8° metal-plated seed beads

9 Picasso with amethyst diamond 10×15mm (small) pressed-glass rectangles

6 Picasso with milky amethyst 11×18mm (large) pressed-glass rectangles

1 natural 15mm "journey" clay irregular round

1 bronze 25×47mm bracelet finding

1 bronze-finish 12×22mm lobster clasp

6 brass 2mm crimp beads

3" (7.5 cm) of gunmetal 20-gauge craft wire

39" (99 cm) of satin copper .018 beading wire

EARRINGS

4 matte fool's gold size 8° metal-plated seed beads

2 Picasso with amethyst diamond 10×15mm pressed-glass rectangles

2 bronze 15mm round star charms

1 pair of antique brass lever-back ear wires

6" (15 cm) of gunmetal 24-gauge craft wire

TOOLS

6 bead stops; chain-nose pliers; round-nose pliers; wire cutters

FINISHED SIZE

Bracelet: 7½" (19 cm)

Earrings (including ear wires): 2¼" (5.5 cm)

TECHNIQUES USED

(see how-to, pp. 97–103)

Crimping; stringing; wrapped loop

BRONZE beads and findings are made of an alloy of copper and tin. Often, beads described as bronze are not pure bronze; rather, they have a rich brown metallic finish similar to that of bronze.

bracelet

1 String the lobster clasp to the center of one 13" (33 cm) piece of beading wire. Use both ends of the wire to string 1 seed bead.

2 Use one end of the previous wire to string 25 seed beads and 3 small pressed-glass rectangles in random order. Place a bead stop on the end of the wire.

3 Use the other end of the previous wire to string 28 seed beads and 2 large pressed-glass rectangles in random order, but with the large rectangles offset from the small rectangles strung in Step 2. Place a bead stop on the end of the wire.

4 Repeat Steps 1–3 twice, for a total of 6 strands. Make sure all of the strands are of equal length; adjust by adding or subtracting seed beads if necessary.

5 Use the craft wire to form a wrapped loop. String the clay round and form a wrapped loop that attaches to one side of the bracelet finding.

6 Remove the bead stop from the strand created in Step 2. String 1 crimp bead and the free wrapped loop from Step 5. Pass back through the crimp bead, snug the beads, and flatten the crimp bead using chain-nose pliers. Trim excess wire.

7 Repeat Step 6 five times, attaching the remaining strands in the order they were created.

To wear, attach the lobster clasp to the free side of the bracelet finding.

earrings

1 Use 3" (7.5 cm) of craft wire to form a wrapped loop that attaches to 1 ear wire. String 1 seed bead, one 10×15mm pressed-glass rectangle, and 1 seed bead; form a wrapped l 1 bronze charm.

2 Repeat Step 1 for a second earring.

{lyrical lariat}

Dark gunmetal chain joins silver and pewter as it weaves its way in and out of this lariat–style necklace.

materials

1 pewter 11×17mm flower bud charm
1 pewter 11×17mm bell drop charm
1 pewter 8×22mm calla lily charm
1 Thai silver 12mm irregular-round ring
1 pewter 38×18mm butterfly connector
5 gunmetal 3×4mm oval jump rings
9" (23 cm) of sterling silver 2×3mm oval chain
11½" (29 cm) of gunmetal 3.5×5mm oval chain
22" (56 cm) of gunmetal 2×3–15mm bar-and-oval chain
23" (58.5 cm) of gunmetal 2–5×3–13mm filigree/twisted bar/oval chain
7½" (19 cm) of sterling silver 24-gauge wire
Oxidizing materials (p. 101)

TOOLS

2 pairs of chain- or flat-nose pliers; round-nose pliers; wire cutters

FINISHED SIZE

25" (63.5 cm)

TECHNIQUES USED

(see how-to, pp. 97–103)
Jump rings; oxidizing metal; wrapped loop

GUNMETAL is a type of bronze, as it is an alloy of copper, tin, and sometimes zinc. Gunmetal beads and findings—whether they are actually made of gunmetal or merely have a gunmetal-like finish—are distinctively steely gray and shiny.

tips *When extended, the center of the lariat opens to 23" (58.5 cm). If you find this to be too small when taking the lariat on and off, simply increase the length of the chains.*

The links of the gunmetal filigree and bar chains used in this project are joined with three oval rings. When cutting these chains, cut the center oval ring.

1 Oxidize the wire; set aside.

2 Use 1 jump ring to attach one end of one 11½" (29 cm) piece of filigree chain to the silver ring. Repeat twice using one 11½" (29 cm) piece of bar chain and the gunmetal oval chain. Use 1 jump ring to attach the free ends of all three chains to the right hole of the connector.

3 Use 1 jump ring to attach one end of each of the following chains to the left hole of the connector: one 10" (25.5 cm) piece of bar chain, one 11" (28 cm) piece of filigree chain, and the silver oval chain. Pass the ends of the chains through the silver ring.

4 Use 2½" (6.5 cm) of wire to form a wrapped loop that attaches to the free end of the silver oval chain; form a second wrapped loop with the same wire that attaches to the flower bud charm. Repeat twice, attaching the bell drop charm to the free end of the filigree chain, and the calla lily charm to the free end of the bar chain.

{we ♥ pewter}

This love-struck necklace is dripping with amazing artisan-made pewter heart beads and lovely blue pearls.

materials

5 Pacific opal 6×4mm crystal rondelles
61 teal 6–7×5mm potato pearls
8 light teal 6–7×5mm potato pearls
1 pewter 15mm (small) vertically drilled heart bead
1 pewter 18×21mm (large) side-drilled heart bead
1 pewter 12×26mm (small) heart pendant
1 pewter 20×30mm (large) heart pendant
2 pewter 15mm heart links
2 pewter 8×31mm oval links
1 pewter 11×24mm heart button
13 pewter 14×6mm bead caps
2 pewter 9×14mm bumpy cones
13 sterling silver 24-gauge 1½" (38mm) ball-end head pins
4 sterling silver 4mm jump rings

6 sterling silver 2mm crimp tubes
6 sterling silver 3mm crimp covers
1½" (3.8 cm) of sterling silver 3mm round chain
5¼" (13.5 cm) of sterling silver 6mm round chain
1⅞" (4.7 cm) of sterling silver 7mm rollo chain
5½" (14 cm) of Thai silver 8mm hammered round chain
8" (20.5 cm) of sterling silver 24-gauge wire
22½" (57 cm) of .018 beading wire
Oxidizing materials (p. 101)

TOOLS

Chain-nose pliers; crimping pliers; round-nose pliers; wire cutters

FINISHED SIZE
Shortest strand: 18½" (47 cm)
Longest strand: 19¾" (50 cm)

TECHNIQUES USED
(see how-to, pp. 97–103)
Crimping; jump rings; oxidizing metal; stringing; wrapped loop

PEWTER beads and findings are made of an alloy of tin (mostly), copper, and antimony. They are sold raw or plated with other metals.

1 Oxidize the head pins, sterling silver wire, jump rings, chain, and crimp covers.

2 Use 1 head pin to string 1 light teal pearl and 1 bead cap; form a wrapped loop. Repeat using the remaining light teal pearls and all the crystals for a total of 13 dangles.

3 Use 2" (5 cm) of sterling silver wire to form a wrapped loop that attaches to one end of one 2¼" (6 mm) piece of 6mm round chain. Use 1 jump ring to attach the other end of the chain to one end of 1 oval link.

4 Use 1 jump ring to attach one end of one 2" (5 cm) piece of hammered round chain to the other end of the previous oval link. Use 1 jump ring to attach the other end of the chain to the left side of 1 heart link.

5 Use 1 jump ring to attach one end of one 3¼" (8.5 cm) piece of 6mm round chain to the right side of the heart link. Use 2" (5 cm) of sterling silver wire to form a wrapped loop that attaches to the other end of the chain. String 1 light teal dangle, 1 teal pearl, 1 crystal dangle, and 1 light teal dangle; form a wrapped loop that attaches to one end of the rollo chain.

6 Use 2" (5 cm) of sterling silver wire to form a wrapped loop that attaches to the other end of the rollo chain. String the large heart bead; form a wrapped loop that attaches to one end of one 3½" (9 cm) piece of hammered round chain. Use 2" (5 cm) of sterling silver wire to form a wrapped loop that attaches to the other end of the hammered round chain.

7 Use 14" (35.5 cm) of beading wire to string 1 crimp tube and the wrapped-loop formed in Step 3; pass back through the tube and crimp. Cover the tube with 1 crimp cover. String 12 teal pearls, 1 light teal dangle, 1 crystal dangle, 1 teal pearl, 1 light teal dangle, 6 teal pearls, the small heart bead, 5 teal pearls, 1 crystal dangle, 1 light teal dangle, 1 teal pearl, 1 crystal dangle, 6 teal pearls, 1 light teal dangle, 1 teal pearl, the large heart pendant, 2 teal pearls, the small heart pendant, 8 teal pearls, 1 crimp tube, and one end of the remaining oval link. Pass back through the tube; crimp and cover.

8 Attach 4½" (11.5 cm) of beading wire to the other end of the previous oval link using 1 crimp tube and 1 crimp cover. String 9 teal pearls, 1 crimp tube, and the left side of the remaining heart link. Pass back through the tube; crimp and cover.

9 Attach 4" (10 cm) of beading wire to the right side of the previous heart link using 1 crimp tube and 1 crimp cover. String 3 teal pearls, 1 light teal dangle, 1 teal pearl, 1 crystal dangle, 1 light teal dangle, 3 teal pearls, 1 crimp tube, and the last wrapped loop formed in Step 6. Pass back through the tube; crimp and cover.

10 Use the wrapped-loop wire from Step 3 to string 1 cone and 1 teal pearl; form a wrapped loop that attaches to the button.

11 Use the wrapped-loop wire from Step 6 to string 1 cone and 1 teal pearl. Form a wrapped loop that attaches to both ends of the 3mm round chain, forming a loop that will fit around the button.

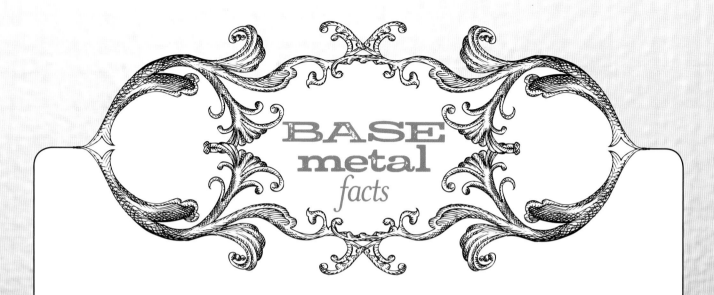

BASE metal *facts*

✦ Copper's chemical symbol, Cu, derives from the word cuprum or cyprium, meaning metal of Cyprus, the land where much of the Roman Empire's copper was mined.

✦ In the United States, in any given year, the amount of copper derived from recycling is almost the same as the amount mined.

✦ The penny was only made of pure copper from 1793 to 1837. Today, a penny contains only 2.5 percent copper (the rest is mostly zinc); however, a nickel contains 75 percent copper and a dime and quarter each contain almost 92 percent copper.

✦ Today, pure copper and more than 400 of its alloys (including brass and bronze) are in use, making copper one of the most used metals in the world.

✦ Although best known for his silverwork, Paul Revere was one of the first American coppersmiths.

✦ People who have allergic reactions to jewelry are usually reacting to the nickel content, which is higher in base-metal products than in high-quality gold and silver products. For mild cases, a thin layer of clear nail polish applied to the jewelry can help.

✦ When copper interacts with skin, it can leave a green residue that is harmless and easy to wash off.

✦ America's brass production got off to a very slow start due to a 1699 law from the English homeland, which prohibited anything, including brass, from being manufactured in the American colonies. Raw materials had to be sent to England, then finished goods were sold back to the colonists.

faux *(& other)* metals

metals, especially precious metals, have been highly valued ever since their discovery thousands of years ago. Apparently even early humans knew a good thing when they saw it! It's interesting to note that civilizations on different continents, discovering the same metals independently of each other, universally put a high price on them—the reason why metals like gold and silver were coined and used as currency for ages, across the globe.

Of course, the high value of metals—again, especially the precious metals—meant that not everybody could afford them, which inspired early bargain hunters (and sometimes crooks) to seek more affordable alternatives. This gave rise to the popularity of metals that look like precious metals (think pyrite, otherwise known as "fool's gold") and metallic finishes on materials that aren't metal at all (think of the metallic-gray comet argent finish on Swarovski crystals or clear pressed-glass beads lined with a glittery paint). Today these materials are esteemed for exactly what they are—beautiful, sparkling, and shiny—not just for being substitutes for real precious metals.

Enameling—a process by which powdered glass is fused to a metal base—produces a product with an appearance that is quite the opposite of a faux metal. In fact, its purpose is to cover the base metal on which it is applied with a smooth finish that is usually very colorful, not metallic. Still, we think it is important to mention enameling, as it was one of the first decorative techniques man used on metal, and enameled beads and findings, such as cloisonné beads, are still very popular today.

for complete NECKLACE instructions

PAGE
66

fool for
gold

PAGE
68

for complete NECKLACE & BRACELET instructions

comet &
cupid

for complete NECKLACE instructions

PAGE 70

gilded
garland

enamel
amour

for complete NECKLACE instructions
PAGE
72

{fool for gold}

Who cares for bona fide gold when you can make a beautiful necklace like this using pyrite rounds, brass chain, and pretty rose-colored beads?

materials

4 vintage rose 6×4mm crystal rondelles

3 lipstick red 4mm (small) fire-polished rounds

1 lipstick red 6mm (large) fire-polished round

1 mottled clear/peach 7mm glass round

4 pale rose 7mm pressed-glass floral rounds

3 finished dangles with peach AB 5×8mm vintage glass teardrops and simple loops

1 finished dangle with clear/opaque rose 16×4mm pressed-glass flower and simple loop

2 peach 8×12mm vintage lampworked drops with bails

1 copper/pink 6×4mm potato pearl

2 silver 8mm irregular pearls

4 rhodonite 5mm (small) rounds

1 rhodonite 7mm (large) faceted round

28 pyrite 10mm rounds

3 rose 9×15mm leaf sequins

4 natural brass 6×3mm blossom bead caps

2 natural brass 15×6mm filigree bead caps

1 gold-plated 17mm textured round box clasp

18 antique brass 24-gauge 1½" (38mm) (short) head pins

1 antique brass 22-gauge 2" (50mm) (long) head pin

7 antique brass 4mm jump rings

2 gold-filled 2mm crimp tubes

2 gold-filled 3mm crimp covers

26½" (67.5 cm) of antique brass 3mm twisted round chain

13¾" (35 cm) of brass 3×5mm oval chain

12⅝" (32 cm) of brass 5×7mm oval chain

14½" (37 cm) of gold satin .018 beading wire

TOOLS

Bead stop; chain-nose pliers; crimping pliers; round-nose pliers; wire cutters

FINISHED SIZE

Shortest strand: 24½" (62 cm)

Longest strand: 27½" (70 cm)

TECHNIQUES USED
(see how-to, pp. 97–103)
Crimping; jump rings; simple loop; stringing; wrapped loop

PYRITE, also known as fool's gold, is a mineral that has often been mistaken for gold. Pyrite beads are beautiful in their own right and are much less expensive than gold beads.

1 Use 1 short head pin to string 1 small lipstick round; form a wrapped loop. Use 1 short head pin to string 1 pale rose round; form a simple loop. Use 1 short head pin to string 1 crystal and 1 blossom bead cap; form a wrapped loop. Use 1 short head pin to string 1 small rhodonite round; form a wrapped loop. Attach 1 jump ring to 1 peach drop.

2 Use the beading wire to string 1 crimp tube and the box half of the clasp; pass back through the tube and crimp. String the lipstick and pale rose dangles formed in Step 1, 1 peach AB teardrop dangle, and the jump ring attached to the peach drop in Step 1. Snug the dangles close to the clasp and cover the crimp tube with 1 crimp cover. String the crystal and the rhodonite dangles from Step 1. String 28 pyrite rounds. Place the bead stop at the end of the wire.

3 Use 1 short head pin to string 1 small rhodonite round; form a simple loop. Use 1 short head pin to string 1 blossom bead cap and the mottled clear/peach round; form a simple loop. Use 1 short head pin to string 1 silver pearl and 1 filigree bead cap; form a simple loop. Use 1 short head pin to string 1 pale rose round; form a simple loop.

4 Remove the bead stop and use the beading wire to string 1 crimp tube, the rhodonite dangle from Step 3, one end of one 11½" (29 cm) piece of round chain, one end of the 5×7mm oval chain, 1 peach drop, one end of the 3×5mm oval chain, and one end of one 14½" (37 cm) piece of round chain. Pass back through the crimp tube; crimp and cover. Attach the remaining dangles from Step 3 and 1 peach AB teardrop dangle to the chains, 1 to 2 chain links below the crimp cover, by opening and closing the simple loops as you would jump rings.

5 Use 1 short head pin to string 1 blossom bead cap and 1 crystal; form a wrapped loop. Use 1 short head pin to string the copper/pink pearl; form a wrapped loop. Use 1 short head pin to string the large lipstick round; form a wrapped loop. Use 1 short head pin to string 1 pale rose round; form a wrapped loop. Use 1 short head pin to string 1 blossom bead cap and the large rhodonite round; form a wrapped loop. *Attach 1 jump ring to 1 sequin; attach a second jump ring to the previous jump ring. Repeat from * once. Use 1 short head pin to string 1 small rhodonite round; form a wrapped loop.

6 Cut the head off the long head pin; form a wrapped loop that attaches to the free ends of the chains. String the first 3 dangles from Step 5. String 1 peach drop, 1 peach AB teardrop dangle, the pale rose dangle from Step 5, 1 crystal, the rhodonite dangle from Step 5, 1 small lipstick round, the second jump ring attached to 1 sequin in Step 5, the pressed-glass flower dangle, the second jump ring attached to 1 sequin in Step 5, 1 small lipstick round, and the small rhodonite dangle from Step 5. Form a wrapped loop that attaches to the tab half of the clasp.

7 Use 1 short head pin to string 1 crystal; form a simple loop. Use 1 short head pin to string 1 pale rose round; form a simple loop. Use 1 short head pin to string 1 small rhodonite round; form a simple loop. Use 1 short head pin to string 1 silver pearl and 1 filigree bead cap; form a simple loop. Attach 1 jump ring to 1 sequin; attach a second jump ring to the previous jump ring.

8 Attach the dangles formed in Step 7 to the chains, 1 to 2 chain links below the first wrapped loop formed in Step 7, opening and closing the simple loops as you would jump rings.

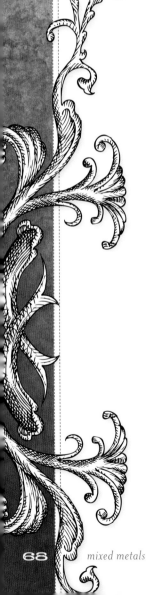

{comet & cupid}

Bows of wire-lace ribbon accent the silvery comet argent Swarovski crystal daisies featured in this necklace and bracelet set.

materials

NECKLACE

2 mint alabaster 3mm crystal rounds

29 mint alabaster 4mm crystal rounds

24 comet argent dark 14mm top-drilled vintage crystal flowers

6 sterling silver 24-gauge 1½" (38mm) ball-end head pins

1 sterling silver 12×50mm ribbon hook-and-eye clasp

2 sterling silver 2mm crimp tubes

2 sterling silver 3mm crimp covers

15" (38 cm) of pale silver 2.5mm wire-lace ribbon

18" (45.5 cm) of sterling silver .021 beading wire

BRACELET

2 mint alabaster 3mm crystal rounds

13 mint alabaster 4mm crystal rounds

8 comet argent dark 14mm top-drilled vintage crystal flowers

6 sterling silver 24-gauge 1½" (38mm) ball-end head pins

1 sterling silver 12×50mm ribbon hook-and-eye clasp

2 sterling silver 2mm crimp tubes

2 sterling silver 3mm crimp covers

3" (7.5 cm) of pale silver 2.5mm wire-lace ribbon

8" (20.5 cm) of sterling silver .021 beading wire

TOOLS

Bead stop; chain-nose pliers; crimping pliers; round-nose pliers; wire cutters

FINISHED SIZE

Necklace: 16¼" (41 cm)

Bracelet: 7" (18 cm)

TECHNIQUES USED

(see how-to, pp. 97–103)

Crimping; knotting; stringing; wrapped loop

SWAROVSKI CRYSTALS can have a metal-like appearance if they are coated with a metallic finish, such as comet argent (silvery), metallic blue, metallic silver, or Dorado (bronzy).

necklace

1 Use the beading wire to string 1 crimp tube and one half of the clasp; pass back through the tube and crimp. Cover the tube with 1 crimp cover.

2 Use the beading wire to string {one 4mm crystal round and 1 crystal flower} twenty-four times. String one 4mm crystal round and 1 crimp tube. Place a bead stop on the end of the wire, leaving a little slack between beads.

3 Use 3" (7.5 cm) of wire-lace ribbon to tie a square knot between 2 crystal flowers, about 3" (7.5 cm) from the attached half of the clasp. Use your fingers to carefully untwist and spread out the wire-lace ribbon. Trim the ribbon ends to about ¾" (2 cm), then roll the ends between your thumb and forefinger to twist. Repeat entire step four times, tying the second knot about 3" (7.5 cm) from the first, the third knot about 2½" (6.5 cm) from the second, the fourth knot about 1" (2.5 cm) from the third, and the fifth knot about 3" (7.5 cm) from the fourth.

4 Remove the bead stop from the end of the wire and string the other half of the clasp. Pass back through the crimp tube; crimp and cover.

5 Use 1 head pin to string one 3mm crystal round; form a wrapped loop that attaches to the loop of one half of the clasp. Repeat twice, using 4mm crystal rounds and attaching the dangles to the same loop. Repeat entire step, attaching the dangles to the loop of the other half of the clasp.

bracelet

1 Use the beading wire to string 1 crimp tube and one half of the clasp; pass back through the tube and crimp. Cover the tube with 1 crimp cover.

2 Use the beading wire to string {one 4mm crystal round and 1 crystal flower} eight times. String one 4mm crystal round and 1 crimp tube. Place a bead stop on the end of the wire, leaving a little slack between beads.

3 Use 3" (7.5 cm) of wire-lace ribbon to tie a square knot between 2 crystal flowers, about 3" (7.5 cm) from the attached half of the clasp. Use your fingers to carefully untwist and spread out the wire-lace ribbon. Trim the ribbon ends to about ¾" (2 cm), then roll the ends between your thumb and forefinger to twist.

4 Remove the bead stop from the end of the wire and string the other half of the clasp. Pass back through the crimp tube; crimp and cover.

5 Use 1 head pin to string one 3mm crystal round; form a wrapped loop that attaches to the loop of one half of the clasp. Repeat twice, using 4mm crystal rounds and attaching the dangles to the same loop. Repeat entire step, attaching the dangles to the loop of the other half of the clasp.

{gilded garland}

The gold-lined and gold-painted pressed-glass flowers and rounds used in this necklace probably contain little real gold, yet the piece has a golden beauty.

materials

16 gold-painted 7mm glass rounds
41 gold-lined clear-and-gold 8mm fluted pressed-glass rounds
8 clear-and-gold 8mm pressed-glass flowers
29 matte blue-and-gold 14mm flat pressed-glass flowers
1 vermeil 20×62mm flower hook-and-eye clasp
4 gold-filled 2mm crimp tubes
4 gold-filled 3mm crimp covers
43½" (110.5 cm) of gold satin .018 beading wire

TOOLS
Crimping pliers; wire cutters

FINISHED SIZE
Shortest strand: 19¾" (50 cm)
Longest strand: 21" (53.5 cm)

TECHNIQUES USED
(see how-to, pp. 97–103)
Crimping; stringing

GLASS beads—for example seed beads and Czech pressed- and fire-polished glass beads—that are lined, painted, or otherwise finished with a metal-colored substance can add great metallic touches to a project.

1 Use 22½" (57 cm) of beading wire to string 1 crimp tube and one half of the clasp; pass back through the tube and crimp. Cover the tube with 1 crimp cover. String 10 clear rounds. String {1 gold round, 1 blue flower, 1 clear round, and 1 blue flower} seven times. String 1 gold round, 10 clear rounds, 1 crimp tube, and the other half of the clasp. Pass back through the tube; crimp and cover.

2 Attach 21" (53.5 cm) of beading wire to one half of the clasp using 1 crimp tube; cover the tube with 1 crimp cover. String 7 clear rounds. String {1 gold round, 1 blue flower, 1 clear flower, and 1 blue flower} four times. String 1 clear flower. String {1 blue flower, 1 gold round, 1 blue flower, and 1 clear flower} three times. String 1 blue flower, 1 gold round, 7 clear rounds, 1 crimp tube, and the other half of the clasp. Pass back through the tube; crimp and cover.

mixing metals

ready for fun? Now that you are familiar with the most common metals and metallic beads used in jewelry making, it's time to mix it up! Today's trend is to combine two or more metals together in a project. This is hard for some people to do—so ingrained is the idea that we should match our metal beads to our metal findings to our chain and wire (to our wristwatch, to our skin tone . . .). Once you've accepted the concept of mixing metals, we promise you'll feel liberated from the matchy-metal mind-set.

The projects that follow, as well as some of the projects within the previous chapters, will hopefully inspire you to combine metals in your own projects. No hard-and-fast rules apply—if anything, we hope our projects prove that *anything goes.*

PAGE **80**

for complete BRACELET & EARRING instructions

feather
your nest

for complete NECKLACE instructions

PAGE 83

adorning
aphrodite

PAGE 84 for complete NECKLACE & BRACELET instructions

secret **garden**

for complete NECKLACE instructions

PAGE
86

memories
of Victoria

{feather your nest}

THAI SILVER + STERLING SILVER + GUNMETAL + BRASS + PEWTER + METALLIC SEED BEADS

A medley of bird-themed beads and charms were carefully collected for this sweet bracelet and matching pair of earrings.

materials

BRACELET

8 metallic frosted clay size 8° seed beads

6 powder blue 4mm (small) potato pearls

5 powder blue 6–8mm (large) potato pearls

3 mottled 13×15mm lampworked glass egg beads

2 antique glass 12mm irregular rings

1 sterling silver/glass 14×32mm "good egg" photo charm

2 natural brass 6×4mm flower spacers

2 pewter 10mm bird-print rounds

4 sterling silver 12×4mm nest beads

2 sterling silver 18×8mm bird beads

5 Thai silver 8×13mm maple leaf charms

4 sterling silver 9×13mm egg-and-nest links

3 raw brass 17×16mm bird links

4 natural brass 17×16mm bird charms

1 sterling silver 20mm bird cutout charm

5 natural brass 7×2mm petal bead caps

1 sterling silver 12×24mm bird toggle clasp

5 natural brass 24-gauge 1½" (38mm) head pins

7 natural brass 22-gauge 2" (50mm) head pins

4 sterling silver 4mm jump rings

1 sterling silver 6mm jump ring

3 antique brass 4mm jump rings

4 antique brass 7mm jump rings

5 natural brass 4mm jump rings

9 natural brass 5mm jump rings

1 natural brass 7mm jump ring

2 natural brass 9.5mm etched jump rings

6½" (16.5 cm [19 links]) of antique brass etched 7×11mm oval chain

6" (15 cm) of gunmetal 24-gauge craft wire

EARRINGS

2 powder blue 4mm (small) potato pearls

2 powder blue 6–8mm (large) potato pearls

2 natural brass 17×16mm bird charms

2 natural brass 7×2mm petal bead caps

4 natural brass 24-gauge 1½" (38mm) head pins

2 natural brass 5mm jump rings

2 natural brass 9.5mm etched jump rings

1 pair of natural brass 16×45mm long ear wires

TOOLS

Wire cutters; chain-nose pliers; round-nose pliers

FINISHED SIZE

Bracelet: 7¼" (18.5 cm)

Earrings (including ear wires): 2½" (6.5 cm)

TECHNIQUES USED

(see how-to, pp. 97–103)

Jump rings; stringing; wrapped loop

bracelet

1 Use 1 natural brass 5mm jump ring to attach the bar (bird) half of the clasp to one end of the chain. This end link of chain will henceforth be referred to as Link 1; the link at the other end of this piece of chain will be referred to as Link 19.

2 Use one 24-gauge head pin to string 1 large pearl and 1 brass bead cap; form a wrapped loop to create a dangle that attaches to Link 1. Repeat four times, attaching the pearl dangles to Links 7, 11, 15, and 18.

3 Use wire cutters to remove the beak-end loop from each raw brass bird link to create raw brass bird charms. Use 1 antique brass 4mm jump ring to attach 1 raw brass bird charm to Link 1; repeat twice, attaching the raw brass bird charms to Links 6 and 16.

4 String 3 small pearls to the center of one 3" (7.5 cm) piece of wire. Twist the wire ends together twice beneath the pearls. Trim one wire end close to the twist; use the remaining wire to string 1 nest bead (top to bottom) and form a wrapped loop.

Press the loop of pearls down into the nest to create a pearl-egg dangle. Repeat entire step for a second pearl-egg dangle. Use 1 natural brass 5mm jump ring to attach 1 pearl-egg dangle to Link 2; repeat, attaching the second pearl-egg dangle to Link 12.

5 Attach 1 natural brass 4mm jump ring to 1 maple leaf charm. Use 1 natural brass 5mm jump ring to attach the previous jump ring to Link 3. Repeat entire step four times, attaching the maple leaf charms to Links 6, 11, 14, and 17.

6 Use wire cutters to remove 1 loop from each sterling silver egg-and-nest link to create sterling silver egg-and-nest charms. Use 1 sterling silver 4mm jump ring to attach 1 sterling silver egg-and-nest charm to Link 3; repeat three times, attaching the sterling silver egg-and-nest charms to Links 9, 15, and 19.

7 Use 1 antique brass 7mm jump ring to string 1 seed bead, 1 natural brass bird charm, and 1 seed bead, then attach the jump ring to Link 4. Repeat three times, attaching the natural brass bird charms to Links 9, 13, and 19.

8 Use one 22-gauge head pin to string 1 lampworked egg; form a wrapped loop to create a lampworked-egg dangle that attaches to Link 4. Repeat twice, attaching the lampworked-egg dangles to Links 10 and 14.

9 Use 1 natural brass 22-gauge head pin to string 1 brass flower spacer and 1 pewter bird-print round; form a wrapped loop that attaches to Link 5. Repeat, attaching the second bird-print round to Link 16.

10 Use 1 natural brass 9.5mm jump ring to attach 1 glass ring to Link 7. Repeat, attaching the second ring to Link 17.

11 Use one 22-gauge head pin to string 1 nest bead and 1 bird bead (both bottom to top); form a wrapped loop to create a bird-and-nest dangle that attaches to Link 8. Repeat, attaching the second bird-and-nest dangle to Link 18.

12 Use the natural brass 7mm jump ring to attach the sterling silver bird cutout charm to Link 10.

13 Use 1 natural brass 5mm jump ring to attach Link 19 (the last chain link) to the ring half of the clasp. Use the 6mm sterling silver jump ring to attach the photo charm to the loop on the ring half of the clasp.

earrings

1 Use 1 head pin to string 1 large pearl and 1 bead cap; form a wrapped loop.

2 Use 1 head pin to string 1 small pearl; form a wrapped loop.

3 Attach one 5mm jump ring to 1 bird charm.

4 Use one 9.5mm jump ring to attach the loop of 1 ear wire to the dangles formed in Steps 1–3, with the bird between the pearls.

5 Repeat Steps 1–4 for a second earring.

{adorning aphrodite}

GOLD-FILLED + GOLD-PLATED + BRASS + METALLIC LUCITE BEADS

Bright brass floral bead caps morph into olive-branch crowns when strung around the rose Lucite beads used in this fit-for-a-goddess necklace. Ambrosia, anyone?

materials

8 erinite 6mm crystal rounds

12 gold-painted 9mm Lucite rounds

16 dusty rose 10×14mm vintage Lucite ovals

1 brass/pink/blue 38×49mm pendant with floral polymer clay–and-crystal inset

20 raw brass 12mm leaf bead caps

1 gold-plated 17mm round box clasp

1 antique brass 3×4mm oval jump ring

2 gold-filled 2mm crimp tubes

2 gold-filled 3mm crimp covers

19½" (49.5 cm) of gold satin .018 beading wire

TOOLS
Crimping pliers; 2 pairs of chain- or flat-nose pliers; wire cutters

FINISHED SIZE
17" (43 cm)

TECHNIQUES USED
(see how-to, pp. 97–103)
Crimping; jump rings; stringing

1 Use the wire to string 1 crimp tube and one half of the clasp. Pass back through the tube and crimp; cover the tube with 1 crimp cover.

2 Before stringing the bead caps, gently shape them so that they will fit snugly over the oval beads when strung. String {1 gold round, 1 oval, 1 bead cap (wide end first), 1 crystal, 1 bead cap (narrow end first), 1 oval, 1 gold round, 1 bead cap (narrow end first), 1 oval, and 1 bead cap (wide end first)} twice. String 1 gold round, 1 oval, 1 bead cap (wide end first), 1 crystal, 1 bead cap (narrow end first), 1 oval, 1 gold round, and 1 crystal.

3 Attach the jump ring to the pendant. String the pendant and 1 crystal. Repeat Step 2, omitting the final crystal. Repeat Step 1 using the other half of the clasp.

{secret garden} STERLING SILVER + BRASS

Here, exquisitely crafted and patinated sterling silver rings are gathered into an enchanting necklace using natural brass jump rings and links of pearls.

materials

NECKLACE

12 peacock 6×5mm potato pearls

10 oxidized sterling silver 13–15mm assorted floral rings

1 sterling silver 22×26mm floral pendant

2 natural brass 7×3mm ornate bead caps

1 sterling silver 6×32mm twig toggle bar

1 sterling silver 22mm flower-and-bird toggle ring

5 natural brass 5mm jump rings

7¼" (18.5 cm) of natural brass 2×3mm peanut chain

7¼" (18.5 cm) of natural brass 4mm flat round chain

13" (33 cm [46 links]) of natural brass 6×10mm etched oval chain with unsoldered links

24" (61 cm) of gunmetal 24-gauge craft wire

BRACELET

6 peacock 6×5mm potato pearls

6 oxidized sterling silver 13–15mm assorted floral rings

1 bronze 14×21mm hook clasp

3" (7.5 cm [11 links]) of natural brass 6×10mm etched oval chain with unsoldered links

12" (30.5 cm) of gunmetal 24-gauge craft wire

TOOLS

2 pairs of chain- or flat-nose pliers; round-nose pliers; wire cutters

FINISHED SIZE

Necklace: 22" (56 cm)

Bracelet: 7½" (19 cm)

TECHNIQUES USED

(see how-to, pp. 97–103)

Jump rings; stringing; wrapped loop

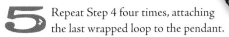

necklace

1 Detach 20 links of etched oval chain by opening the links as you would jump rings. Set aside.

2 Attach 1 jump ring to the toggle ring.

3 Use 1 jump ring to attach one end of one 3⅝" (9 cm) piece of round chain, one 3⅝" (9 cm) piece of peanut chain, and one 3⅝" (9 cm) piece (13 links) of oval chain to the previous jump ring. Use 2" (5 cm) of wire to form a wrapped loop that attaches to the free ends of the previous chains. String 1 bead cap (wide end first) and 1 pearl; form a wrapped loop. Gently squeeze the bead cap so that it tightens around the chains.

4 Use 1 oval link set aside from Step 1 to attach the previous wrapped loop to 1 silver ring. Attach 1 oval link to the other side of the silver ring. Use 2" (5 cm) of wire to form a wrapped loop that attaches to the previous oval link; string 1 pearl and form a wrapped loop.

5 Repeat Step 4 four times, attaching the last wrapped loop to the pendant.

6 Attach 1 jump ring to the center of the twig bar. Attach 1 jump ring to the previous jump ring. Repeat Steps 3–5 for the other half of the necklace.

bracelet

1 Detach 11 links of the chain by opening the links as you would jump rings; set aside.

2 Use 2" (5 cm) of wire to form a wrapped loop that attaches to the hook clasp. String 1 pearl and form a wrapped loop.

3 Use 1 oval link set aside from Step 1 to attach the previous wrapped loop to 1 silver ring. Attach 1 oval link to the other side of the previous silver ring. Use 2" (5 cm) of wire to form a wrapped loop that attaches to the previous oval link; string 1 pearl and form a wrapped loop.

4 Repeat Step 3 four times. Use 1 oval link to attach the previous wrapped loop to 1 silver ring.

To wear, attach the hook clasp to the final silver ring.

{memories of victoria}

STERLING SILVER + SILVER-PLATED + COPPER + BRONZE + GUNMETAL + BRASS + METALLIC GLASS BEADS

By using antique and antique-looking beads and a locket with a faux patina, we gave this bead-encrusted necklace the appearance of an updated heirloom.

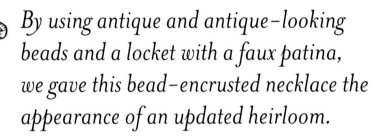

materials

- 11 silver-lined clear-and-silver 8mm fluted pressed-glass rounds
- 18 dark teal/bronze 9×5mm fire-polished rondelles
- 4 matte blue-and-gold 14mm flat pressed-glass flowers
- 13 mottled light blue-and-clear 16mm glass rounds
- 8 light blue AB 12×10mm pressed-glass bellflowers
- 5 finished dangles with glass faux-pearl 11×24mm teardrops and simple loops
- 4 brushed copper 9×12mm teardrops
- 1 brass 33×47mm filigree locket
- 4 bronze 10mm filigree rounds
- 4 silver-plated 10×18mm feather charms
- 6 teal 10–15×16–24mm assorted vintage enameled-metal filigree charms
- 1 bronze finish 15×25mm lobster clasp
- 8 natural brass 6×3mm blossom bead caps
- 10 natural brass 9×5mm foliage bead caps
- 26 natural brass 15×6mm filigree bead caps
- 38 brass 22-gauge 2" (50mm) head pins
- 19 natural and/or antique brass 7mm jump rings
- 4 sterling silver 2mm crimp tubes
- 4 natural brass 4×2mm spacers/crimp covers
- 17" (43 cm) of antique brass .024 beading wire
- 4" (10 cm) of gunmetal 20-gauge craft wire
- 8" (20.5 cm [20 links]) of bronze finish 11×15mm decorative heavy oval chain
- Metal painting materials (p. 102)

TOOLS

Chain-nose pliers; crimping pliers; flat-nose pliers; round-nose pliers; wire cutters

FINISHED SIZE
21½" (54.5 cm)

TECHNIQUES USED
(see how-to, pp. 97–103)

Crimping; jump rings; painting metals; stringing; wrapped loop

1 Paint the locket (p. 102).

2 Use the beading wire to string 2 crimp tubes and one end of the chain. Pass back through the crimp tubes and crimp. String 2 spacers/crimp covers over the crimp tubes. String {1 filigree bead cap (narrow end first), 1 mottled glass round, 1 filigree bead cap (wide end first) and 1 clear-and-silver round} twelve times, omitting the final clear-and-silver round. String 2 crimp tubes and the lobster clasp. Pass back through the tubes and crimp. Trim excess wire and cover the crimp tubes with 2 spacers/crimp covers.

3 Attach the lobster clasp to the free end of the chain. This end link of chain will henceforth be referred to as Link 1; the link on the other end of this piece of chain will be referred to as Link 20.

4 Use 1 jump ring to attach 1 filigree charm to Link 1. Repeat five times, attaching filigree charms to Links 5, 7, 11, 15, and 17.

5 Use 1 head pin to string 1 fire-polished rondelle and 1 foliage bead cap; form a wrapped loop that attaches to Link 1. Repeat nine times, attaching foliage-bead-cap dangles to Links 3, 5, 7, 9, 11, 13, 15, 17, and 19.

6 Use 1 head pin to string 1 matte blue flower; form a wrapped loop that attaches to Link 1. Repeat three times, attaching matte blue flowers to Links 5, 11, and 17.

7 Use 1 head pin to string 1 filigree round; form a wrapped loop that attaches to Link 2. Repeat three times, attaching filigree rounds to Links 6, 12, and 16.

8 Use 1 head pin to string 1 fire-polished rondelle and 1 blossom bead cap; form a wrapped loop that attaches to Link 2. Repeat seven times, attaching blossom-bead-cap dangles to Links 4, 6, 8, 12, 14, 16, and 18.

9 Use 1 jump ring to attach 1 faux-pearl dangle to Link 2. Repeat four times, attaching faux-pearl dangles to Links 6, 12, 16, and 19.

10 Use 1 head pin to string 1 copper teardrop; form a wrapped loop that attaches to Link 3. Repeat three times, attaching copper-teardrop dangles to Links 9, 15, and 19.

11 Use 1 jump ring to attach 1 feather charm to Link 3. Repeat three times, attaching feather charms to Links 9, 13, and 19.

12 Use 1 head pin to string 1 pressed-glass bellflower (wide end first); form a wrapped loop. Repeat for another bellflower dangle. Use 1 jump ring to attach both bellflower dangles to Link 4. Repeat entire step three times, attaching 2 bellflower dangles to Links 8, 14, and 18.

13 Use the gunmetal wire to form a wrapped loop that attaches to Link 10. String 1 filigree bead cap (narrow end first), 1 mottled glass round, and 1 bead cap (wide end first); form a wrapped loop that attaches to the locket.

glossary of terms

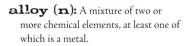

alloy (n): A mixture of two or more chemical elements, at least one of which is a metal.

antique brass (n): A type of brass distinguished by its aged appearance, which is somewhere between the shininess of raw brass and the darkness of natural brass.

antimony (n): A chemical element (symbol Sb) that is one of the alloys that composes pewter.

base metal (n): Any metal other than a precious metal, often plated with a precious metal, such as copper, bronze, brass, gunmetal, and pewter.

brass (n): An alloy of copper and zinc, considered a base metal.

bronze (adj): A metallic dark brown color.

bronze (n): An alloy of copper and tin, considered a base metal.

bronze age (n): A broad term for the period (beginning about 3000 B.C.) when man used bronze to make tools and weapons (as opposed to the preceding Stone Age and succeeding Iron Age).

chemical element (n): A substance that cannot be broken down into simpler substances using chemical means; often displayed in a periodic table. Ninety-four of these elements occur naturally on earth.

cloisonné beads (n): Beads made using an enameling technique whereby enamel is placed into cells, which are made with strips of metal.

comet argent (n): A finish applied to Swarovski crystals that give them a metallic silver look.

copper (n): A chemical element (symbol Cu) with a reddish orange hue that is considered a base metal, though it is not an alloy of other base metals.

corrode (v): To eat or wear away.

dorado (n): A finish applied to Swarovski crystals, which gives them a metallic bronze look.

ductile (adj): Ability to be drawn into fine wires without breaking.

enamel (n): Powdered glass fused to a metal base, resulting in a colorful finish.

enamel (v): To fuse powdered glass to a metal base.

faux metal (n): A material that looks like a metal.

fineness/purity (n): Amount of pure precious metal in an alloy; the higher the amount of precious metal, the purer or finer the alloy.

fine silver (n): Silver that is 99.9 percent pure.

gold (n): A chemical element (symbol Au) and one of the precious metals.

gold-filled (adj): Made of a base metal that is bonded with a layer of gold that must be at least 10k and equal to at least $1/20$ of the whole item's weight.

gold-plated (adj): Bonded with a thin layer of gold that must be at least 10k.

gold-plated German metal beads (n): Beads made of a tin base (or findings with a brass base) that are bonded with a layer of 22k gold.

gunmetal (n): A type of bronze, being an alloy of copper, tin, and sometimes a small amount of zinc, that is considered a base metal.

gunmetal (adj): Steely gray and shiny.

karat (n): The designation of fineness for gold, whereby pure gold is designated as 24k gold. The word karat comes from the Arabic word for the carob seed, which was used in ancient times to measure the weight of gold.

luster (n): Surface radiance or shine.

malleable (adj): Ability to be beaten or pressed into various shapes without breaking.

metal (n): A chemical element or alloy that is opaque, dense, ductile, conductive of heat and electricity, and lustrous.

metallic (adj): Having a lustrous appearance similar to a metal.

metallic blue (n): A finish applied to Swarovski crystals, which gives them a metallic blue look.

metallic silver (n): A finish applied to Swarovski crystals, which gives them a metallic silver look.

natural brass (n): A type of brass with a dark antiqued finish.

pewter (n): An alloy of tin (mostly), copper, and antimony that is considered a base metal.

precious metal (n): The metallic chemical elements that are of high economic value and are usually rare, such as gold, silver, platinum, and palladium.

precious metal clay (n): A substance that, when heated at a high temperature, releases stabilizers and leaves behind only pure silver. Beads made of PMC are considered fine silver.

pyrite (n): A mineral, also known as fool's gold, which has often been mistaken for gold.

raw brass (n): Brass with a shiny, goldlike appearance.

rose gold (n): A gold alloy that contains a relatively high percentage of copper (thus the reddish tint) and usually some silver.

rose gold vermeil (adj): Having a sterling (or fine) silver base that is bonded with a layer of rose gold.

rust (v): To become corroded by air and moisture.

silver (n): A chemical element (symbol Ag) and the most plentiful and inexpensive of the precious metals.

silver-plated (adj): Made of a base metal that is coated with a thin layer of fine silver.

sterling silver (n): Silver that contains 925 parts silver to 75 parts copper, long considered a standard for silver. All goods sold as sterling silver must have a "925" stamp.

tarnish (v): To dull, discolor, stain.

thai silver (n): Silver produced by the people of the Karen hill tribe in Thailand that is 95 to 99 percent pure silver.

vermeil (adj): Having a sterling (or fine) silver base that is bonded with a layer of gold that must be at least 10k.

This handy guide to beading, wireworking, and working with metal will tell you all you need to know to become a well-educated jewelry maker. For detailed information and fun facts about the metals featured in this book, see chapter and project introductions.

beading & wireworking 101

beads

CLAY ↓

Polymer clay: Beads made from a type of clay that can be baked at a lower temperature than ceramic beads and thus don't require a kiln. Though technically a plastic, polymer clay looks like ceramic.

polymer

ceramic

PMC

Ceramic: Clay beads that have been fired at a high temperature and are often coated with a decorative glaze and/or handpainted designs.

Precious metal clay (PMC): Beads formed from a claylike material that becomes 99.9 percent fine silver when fired.

CRYSTALS ↑

Leaded glass beads that, more often than not, are produced by the Austrian company Swarovski. Crystals come in various sizes, shapes, and colors and are almost always faceted. Use beading wire or braided beading thread when stringing crystals as the sharp edges of the holes in the beads may cut through nylon beading thread.

GLASS →

Seed beads: Tiny glass beads available in endless colors and finishes. Most are produced in Japan or the Czech Republic.

Aught describes a seed bead's size and is represented by a small degree sign.

They generally range from size 20° to 6° (the smaller the number, the larger the bead). The exact origin of this symbol is unknown.

Fire-polished: Glass beads (generally from the Czech Republic) that are faceted to catch light and often have a surface finish applied to them for extra sparkle. Because of the large number of facets, fire-polished rounds tend to be slightly oval in shape. Fire-polished beads are an affordable alternative to crystals.

seed

lampworked

fire-polished

pressed-glass

Pressed-glass: Glass beads (also generally from the Czech Republic) that are made by pressing glass into molds. They come in a variety of colors, sizes, and shapes, including rounds, flowers, leaves, and more.

Lampworked: Artisan-made beads created by working hot glass rods over a flame (in the old days, a lamp; today, a propane torch).

crystal

freshwater

PEARLS ↑

Freshwater: Pearls cultured in inland lakes and rivers. These are genuine pearls cultivated by inserting irritants into farmed oysters to stimulate their production; nacre coating is formed around these irritants, resulting in unevenly sized pearls. Freshwater pearls are offered in innumerable sizes, shapes, and colors.

Crystal: Made by Swarovski, these imitation pearls have a crystal core coated with a thick pearl-like substance. They are perfectly shaped and have a weight similar to that of genuine pearls.

bead shapes

Bead shapes vary greatly. Here are some of the most common bead shapes known to beaders. Don't hesitate to experiment with a variety of shapes in your own designs.

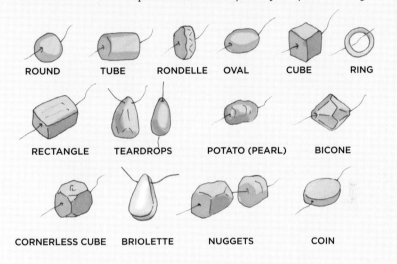

ROUND   TUBE   RONDELLE   OVAL   CUBE   RING

RECTANGLE   TEARDROPS   POTATO (PEARL)   BICONE

CORNERLESS CUBE   BRIOLETTE   NUGGETS   COIN

bead sizes

Beads are measured in millimeters, except for seed beads, which have their own sizing systems (see seed beads on p. 90). Bead measurements are given as width by length.

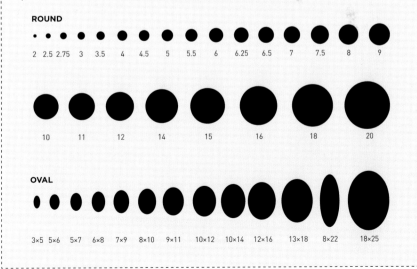

ROUND

2 2.5 2.75 3 3.5 4 4.5 5 5.5 6 6.25 6.5 7 7.5 8 9

10 11 12 14 15 16 18 20

OVAL

3×5 5×6 5×7 6×8 7×9 8×10 9×11 10×12 10×14 12×16 13×18 8×22 18×25

PLASTIC ↓

Lucite: A plastic created in the 1930s for use in fighter planes and later used for costume jewelry. Jewelry made of this material was most popular in the early 1950s, and although the material is still being produced today, most of the beads on the market are from factories that closed in the 1970s, making the pieces truly vintage. Beads made of this material are vibrantly colored and available in countless shapes, sizes, and colors.

SEMIPRECIOUS STONES ↓

A term that generally refers to natural minerals (i.e., peridot), rocks (i.e., lapis lazuli), and organic materials (i.e., amber and jet). Semiprecious stone beads are found in countless varieties, however, the stones used in this book include aquamarine, rhodonite,

and pyrite. Take care to string large stone beads on strong beading wire as they can be heavy.

VINTAGE ↑

Beads that are old (but may not appear so) and are usually collector's items. Often vintage molds are purchased by contemporary companies so that vintage designs can be produced again.

findings

Jewelry components, often made of metal, that, whether functional or decorative, pull jewelry projects together. The following are the most common findings used in jewelry making.

BEAD CAPS ↓

A decorative metal cup-shaped element strung snug up to the top or bottom of a bead.

CHAIN ↑

Chain is available in a multitude of finishes, sizes, and shapes, including oval, round, short-and-long, even filigree. Most often the links are soldered and must be cut open. However, if the links are already split, they can be opened like jump rings and no links will be wasted. Chain is measured by the size of its links.

CHARMS ↑

A tiny (usually metal) pendant, often used in charm bracelets, as pendants, or as embellishments. They are hung by a loop on one end.

hook-and-eye

S-hook

toggle

lobster

box

CLASPS ↑

Toggle clasps: These clasps have a bar on one side and a ring on the other. Since the bar must pass through the ring when attaching the necklace or bracelet, be sure to string at least ½" (1.3 cm [or a little more than half the length of the bar]) of small beads at the end of the strand before the bar.

S-hook clasps: Made of an S-shaped wire permanently attached to a jump ring on one side, the S closes through a second jump ring on the opposite side.

Box clasps: Shaped like a rectangle, square, or circular box on one end, these clasps have a bent metal tab on the other end that snaps into the box under its own tension. The tops often have stone, glass, pearl, or other decorative inlays and the ends often have numerous metal loops to accommodate multiple strands.

Lobster clasps: These (often small) closures open and close like a claw and are great for connecting jewelry to chain.

Hook-and-eye clasps: These clasps have a J-shaped hook on one side that connects to a loop (or ring) on the opposite side.

CONES →

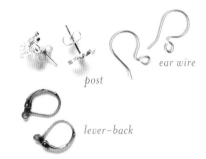

Cylindrical findings that taper to a point at one end. Cones are great for neatly gathering the ends of multiple strands: Use at least 2" (5 cm) of gauged wire to form a wrapped loop that attaches to your design's strands. Use the wire end to string the wide end of the cone to cover the ends of the strands, then form a second wrapped loop that attaches to a clasp.

CONNECTORS ↑

A connector or link (often metal) has a loop on each end and is used to join one strand, thread, chain, etc., to another.

CRIMPING FINDINGS →

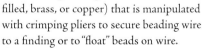

cover

tube

bead

Crimp tube: A small cylinder of metal (most often sterling silver, gold-filled, brass, or copper) that is manipulated with crimping pliers to secure beading wire to a finding or to "float" beads on wire.

Crimp bead: This finding serves the same purpose as a crimp tube, but is round, and is flattened using chain- or flat-nose pliers.

Crimp cover: A hollow, partially opened C-shaped bead that wraps around a crimp tube or bead to conceal it, giving jewelry a clean finishing touch.

post

ear wire

lever-back

EARRING FINDINGS ↑

Earring findings, the foundations for earrings, are available in these varieties and more: Chandelier, ear wire (also called hook), hoop, lever-back, and post.

FILIGREES ↓

Filigrees are metal components, such as pendants, beads, and connectors, that feature lacelike ornamental openwork. They are available in numerous metals and finishes.

PENDANTS ↑

A pendant is a suspended ornament, usually the focal piece of a necklace.

PINS ↓

Flat-end head pin: The most common style of head pin. When a bead is strung on one, the flat end sits flush against the hole in the bead. If the gauge is not indicated, it is probably 24-gauge; this gauge is strong yet thin enough to accommodate most beads. Head pins are often used to make earrings and can also be used to wire wrap a dangle to a piece of jewelry.

Ball-end head pin: A pin with a round, instead of flat, end.

decorative head pin: A pin with a decorative end, such as a flower, leaf, or teardrop.

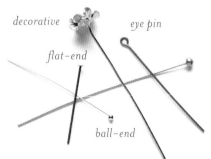

decorative

eye pin

flat-end

ball-end

Eye pin: This pin works like a head pin, but has a simple loop at one end so that it may be connected to other design elements.

RINGS & BAILS ↓

Jump ring: A small, usually circular or oval piece of wire used to connect jewelry components to each other. Most jump rings are unsoldered, meaning they are severed and can be opened and closed to string components; some are soldered, meaning they cannot be opened and closed, only linked to.

Bail: A general term for the hanger at the top of a pendant, bead, or finding made to attach it to your piece of jewelry. If a bead or pendant does not come with an attached bail, you can either make your own with wire (see page 100) or buy a premade bail.

SPACERS →

A small bead, often round or rondelle, strung between other larger beads to set them apart and draw attention to them.

stringing tools & materials

BEADING WIRE ↑

Strong, flexible wire that is made of multiple thin steel wires that have been coated with nylon. The more strands of wires used, the more flexible the beading wire. This wire is most commonly secured with crimp tubes and beads. We like to use .014 or .015 for lighter projects (best used with 1mm or 1×2mm crimp tubes and Micro crimping pliers) and .019 and .018 for heavier projects (best used with 2mm crimp tubes); see the box on p. 97 for more information about choosing the right crimp tube for the right wire.

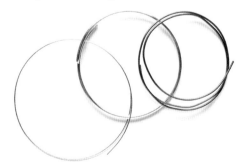

METAL WIRE ↑

Hard, half-hard, and dead-soft: These terms refer to the "temper" (hardness or softness) of the wire. Half-hard is our favorite tem per and the one most commonly used for creating wrapped-loop links and dangles. In this book, half-hard wire should be assumed unless an alternate hardness is indicated. Wire is naturally "work hardened" through manipulation; if overworked, the wire will become brittle and break.

Craft wire: Copper wire that has been permanently coated with a colored finish. This wire tends to be soft and the color coating can chip, so use light pressure when making simple and wrapped loops.

GAUGE

The term used to indicated the thickness of the wire. Our favorite gauges are 22- or 24-gauge wire (the lower the number, the thicker the wire). 22-gauge is about 0.6mm thick and 24-gauge is about 0.5mm thick.

10	━━━━━━━ ●
12	━━━━━━ ●
14	━━━━━ ●
16	━━━━ ●
18	━━━ ●
20	━━ ●
22	── •
24	── •
26	── •
28	── •

RIBBON ↑

A narrow strip of fabric, often silk or satin. Ribbon is a great way to incorporate a different stringing material or embellishment into your designs.

BEAD STOPS ↑

Springlike or cliplike findings that temporarily snap onto the end of beading wire to prevent spills while stringing.

DESIGN BOARD ↓

A valuable tool that prevents beads from rolling around your work surface. Most have semicircle grooves in the shape of a necklace or bracelet that allow you to visualize a design before it is strung. Although this is not a required tool, you may find it very helpful.

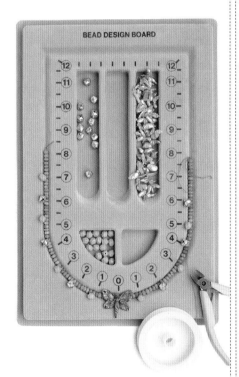

BEAD DESIGN BOARD

WIRE OR FLUSH CUTTERS →

Tools used to cut both gauged wire and beading wire. Their sharp edges ensure that no burrs are left on the trimmed ends of the wire.

CHAIN- & FLAT-NOSE PLIERS →

Tools essential for opening and closing jump rings and manipulating wire. The inside jaws of both are flat and smooth. However, the outside edges of chain-nose pliers are round on the top and bottom, and flat-nose pliers (shown) are flat on both edges. Chain-nose pliers taper toward the tip, making them great for working with small links of chain and in other small spaces; flat-nose pliers are wider, giving you more gripping power.

ROUND-NOSE PLIERS →

Tools used to make loops and curls with wire. Their conical jaws taper toward the tip, creating many loop-size options. If a large loop is desired, position wire near the base of the jaw; for small loops, work the wire at the tips.

CRIMPING PLIERS →

Pliers that have two notches used to secure crimp tubes on beading wire: one notch is used to flatten crimp tubes and the other is used to fold the tube in half. They are available in three sizes: generally Micro pliers are used when working with 1mm wide tubes, regular for 2mm wide tubes, and Mighty for 3mm tubes.

how-to

In this section you will find easy-to-follow instructions for all the beading and wireworking techniques used in this book.

STRINGING

Simply use a wire (beading or gauged) or a needle and thread to pick up beads and gather them into a strand.

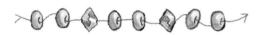

Pass through vs. pass back through: Pass through means to pass through a bead a second time, moving the wire (or needle) in the same direction as the first pass. To pass back through, move the wire (or needle) in the opposite direction as the first pass.

CRIMPING

This is a technique by which you mold a crimp tube or bead around beading wire using crimping or flat-nose pliers. Most often this technique is used to attach a clasp to a piece of jewelry, thereby creating a secure finish.

Crimp tubes: Use beading wire to string 1 crimp tube, pass through a finding, and pass back through the tube, leaving a ¼ to ½" (6 mm to 1.3 cm) tail.

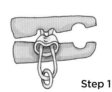

Step 1

Make sure the wires do not cross inside the tube. Pinch the tube into a U shape, using the back notch of the crimping pliers **(Step 1)**. Each wire should now be contained in its own chamber.

Step 2

Turn the pinched tube 90° and use the front notch of the crimping pliers to fold it into a cylinder **(Step 2)**. Trim excess wire.

Crimp beads: Repeat as for crimp tubes, but instead of crimping with crimping pliers, flatten the bead using chain- or flat-nose pliers. *Note:* Although some manufacturers do recommend using crimping pliers to crimp their crimp beads, all of the crimp beads in this book are flattened using chain- or flat-nose pliers; crimping pliers are reserved for use with crimp tubes.

Crimp covers: Hold the cover in the front notch of the crimping pliers, position it over a crimped crimp tube, and gently squeeze the pliers to form the C-shaped finding into a round bead. For a perfectly round crimp cover, rotate the pliers around the cover just before you pinch the cover completely closed. It is a good idea to make sure the piece of jewelry you are working on is lying facedown; that way the seam of the crimp tube will be on the underside of the piece.

THE RIGHT CRIMP TUBE FOR THE RIGHT WIRE

Check with the manufacturer of your wire for a complete list of what crimp tubes to pair with what beading-wire sizes and how many strands of that wire a single crimp tube can accommodate. Here are a few general guidelines for the most commonly used sizes:

+ The 1x1mm crimp tubes are best used with 1 strand of size .010 to .019 wire and Micro crimping pliers.

+ The 2x2mm crimp tubes are best used with 1 strand of size .014 to .024 wire (though we prefer to use no less than .018 for this size of crimp tube) and regular crimping pliers.

+ The 3x3mm crimp tubes are best used with 1 strand of size .024 to .026 wire and Mighty crimping pliers.

JUMP RINGS

Using two pairs of chain- or flat-nose pliers (round-nose pliers usually leave marks) or a combination of the two, open and close jump rings by twisting the sides of the jump ring in opposite directions, one side straight toward you and one side straight away from you (pulling the ends straight away from each other will distort the ring). String whatever you wanted to attach to the jump ring, then twist the sides of the jump ring in opposite directions to close.

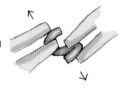

Stringing with a jump ring: For a quick and simple dangle, open a jump ring wide and string a bead before closing (this works best with jump rings made of thin wire and beads with larger holes).

SIMPLE LOOP

This is the preferred loop for creating a dangle with a bead that is not heavy. It can be opened and closed like a jump ring, so if you want to change its placement, you can do so easily.

Use chain- or flat-nose pliers to form a 90° bend ½ to 1" (1.3 to 2.5 cm) from the end of your wire.

Step 1

Imagine the size of the loop you would like to make, then place the nose of the round-nose pliers on the short wire at a distance from the bend that equals about half the circumference of the loop you imagined. Roll the pliers toward the bend, then use your finger to wrap the short wire the rest of the way around the pliers **(Step 1)**, adjusting the pliers as needed, until the short wire crosses the bend and the base of the loop **(Step 2)**.

Step 2

While still holding the loop in the pliers, adjust the wire below the bend as needed to restore the 90° angle. Trim the wire next to the bend.

Double simple loop: Begin as if making a basic simple loop, but bend the wire 1 to 2" (2.5 to 5 cm) from the end. After forming the loop, continue to wrap the wire around the pliers for a second time, creating a second loop. Trim the wire at the point where it crosses the bend.

Simple-loop link: This is a piece of wire with simple loops on each end for attaching to other loops, chains, clasps, etc.

Form a simple loop at one end of the wire and string a bead.

To make the 90° bend close to the bead, snug the bead down to the first loop and use your fingers (or chain- or flat-nose pliers) to fold the wire over the bead.

Form a second simple loop to complete the link.

Simple-loop dangle: Use a head pin to string one or more beads and form a simple loop.

WRAPPED LOOP

This sturdy loop is preferable when creating a dangle or link that is heavy or will incur strain. Use chain- or flat-nose pliers to form a 90° bend 1 to 2" (2.5 to 5 cm) from the end of your wire.

Make a simple loop, but do not trim the tail. Grasp the loop with chain-nose pliers **(Step 1)**. Use your fingers or hold the end of the wire with chain- or flat-nose pliers to wrap the tail down the neck of the main wire at the base of the loop for about two or three wraps **(Step 2)**. Trim the wire at the end of the last wrap. For tight wraps, think of pulling the wire away from the loop as you wrap.

Once you've trimmed the wire after making wraps, press the end down with either flat-nose pliers or the front notch of crimping pliers so the end doesn't stick out.

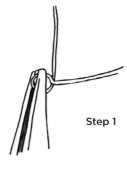

Step 1

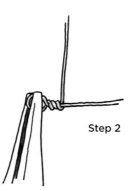

Step 2

Double-wrapped loop: Begin as if making a wrapped loop, but instead of trimming the wire tail after two or three wraps, continue wrapping back up and over the previous wraps and toward the loop.

Wrapped-loop link: This is a piece of wire with wrapped loops on each end for attaching to other loops, chains, clasps, etc. Form a wrapped loop at one end of the wire and string a bead. Snug the bead down to the first loop and grasp the wire just above the bead using the tip of your chain-nose pliers **(Step 1)**.

Make a 90° bend **(Step 2)** and form a wrapped loop as before to complete the link.

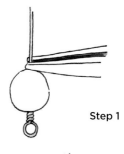

Step 1

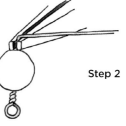

Step 2

Connecting a wrapped loop: Make a basic wrapped loop, but before wrapping the tail down the neck of the main wire, string the chain link, clasp, link, or other finding **(Step 1)**.

Grasp the loop with the tip of the chain-nose pliers, holding the strung finding out of the way **(Step 2)** and wrap the tail down the neck of the main wire as before.

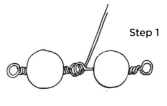

Step 1

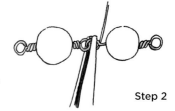

Step 2

Wrapped-loop dangle: Use a head pin to string one or more beads and form a wrapped loop.

Wrapped-loop bail: Use 4½ to 5" (11.5 to 12.5 cm) of wire to string 1 bead (usually a teardrop or briolette), positioning the bead so that it is about 1½ to 2" (3.8 to 5 cm) from one end of the wire. Bend both wire ends toward the center top of the bead, forming a triangle. Use chain-nose pliers to bend the long wire straight up at the top of the bead **(Step 1)**.

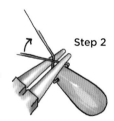

Step 1

Wrap the short wire around the long wire; if you have trouble holding the wires and bead while wrapping, swing the top of the bead out of the triangle formed and hold the triangle with round-nose pliers **(Step 2)**.

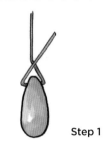

Step 2

Hold the first wraps with the chain-nose pliers and bend the remaining wire down to one side at a 90° angle. Use the round-nose pliers to form a loop **(Step 3)**.

Hold the loop in chain-nose pliers and wrap the wire down over the first wraps. Trim excess wire.

For a decorative bail, continue to wrap over the top of the bead. Trim excess wire **(Step 4)**. *Note:* You will want to start with at least 10" (25.5 cm) of wire when making a decorative bail.

Step 3

Step 4

BEADING AND WIREWORKING TIPS

+ If you need just a small amount of wire to make a link and don't have the color or gauge of wire that you need, simply cut the end off of a long head pin (as we did on p. 33).

+ Always be sure to check that the head or eye pins you are buying are the correct gauge to fit through your bead(s). Err on the side of longer head pins—they are easier to work with, and you can often recycle the scrap metal.

+ If the last bead or bead cap strung on a head pin or link has a large hole that might slip over the finished wrapped loop, form a double-wrapped loop.

+ Double-check that jump rings and simple loops are completely closed before stringing them on thin beading wire, or else they may slip off. To prevent this, form a double simple or wrapped loop instead.

+ Sort through and discard irregular stones before beginning every project, and purchase more than you think you need because you may find that the holes in many of the beads are too small or poorly drilled.

KNOTTING

This technique requires only scissors; no other tools are needed. The steps for creating the two different types of knots used in this book are described below.

Overhand knot: This is the most basic knot, though it is not the most secure. Make a loop with your stringing material by crossing the left end over the right. Pass the left end through the loop from the back so that it resembles a pretzel. Pull the thread tight.

Square knot: Working with two cords (or threads), cross the right end over the left end and wrap it around the left cord as if making an overhand knot. Make an overhand knot by passing the left end over the right and pull the threads tight.

oxidizing metal

Most metal will change color over time since oxidation is the natural aging that occurs when metal is exposed to air. To speed this process, you can chemically alter the color of your metal using one of the following methods. To color sterling silver and copper, use liver of sulfur, patina, or a hard-boiled egg. To color brass, use patina (liver of sulfur will only slightly dull bright brass). Gold-filled findings and most coated copper wire (called "craft wire") cannot be oxidized.

Always wear gloves, work in a well-ventilated area (liver of sulfur has an unpleasant odor, but it quickly dissipates), and carefully read manufacturer's directions when using chemicals. Wash all metal to be colored with soap and water and handle pieces with gloves on after washing. For ease of dipping, use 12" (30.5 cm) of sewing or beading thread to string the finding or bead(s) you wish to oxidize, then use the ends to tie an overhand knot. If coloring small items that cannot be strung (such as crimp covers), you will need to drop them in the solution and then quickly scoop them out with a plastic spoon. Another method to color small items is to place them on a paper towel and brush them with the solution; this method, however, often results in uneven coloring. See a list of the other materials needed on p. 102.

After coloring your metal using one of the methods explained in detail below and on p. 102, begin the finishing process by removing any threads you used to suspend the pieces. If desired, use a polishing cloth to buff the pieces and to lighten the color. If you wish to remove a large amount of color, polish with #0000 (extra-fine) steel wool. See the Caring for Metals section on p. 103 for tips on preserving the colors you achieved.

Patina: Pour a small amount of patina into a disposable container. For allover color, dip the entire piece into the patina.

For stripes, slowly lower the piece partially into the liquid and hold the piece still. Once the desired color is achieved, rinse off the pieces in cold water. (Novacan Black Patina, most often used to color lead solder, can be purchased at stained-glass-supply stores.)

Liver of sulfur: Unlike patina, this can produce colors other than black. Though liver of sulfur is available in a solution, we prefer to use the dry nuggets because they allow us to have better control over the strength of the solution.

oxidizing materials

{what you need}

PATINA

Gloves

Patina (we use Novacan Black Patina)

Disposable container (glass or plastic)

Thread or plastic spoon

Clean cotton or paper towel

Polishing cloth and steel wool (optional)

LIVER OF SULFUR

Gloves

Liver of sulfur

Disposable container (glass or plastic)

Thread and plastic spoon

Baking soda

Clean cotton or paper towel

Polishing cloth and steel wool (optional)

HARD-BOILED EGG

Airtight container with lid (glass or plastic)

Hard-boiled egg

Fork

Thread

Water for rinsing

Clean cotton or paper towel

Polishing cloth and steel wool (optional)

Mix nuggets in hot (almost boiling) water according to manufacturer's directions in a disposable container; mix a weak solution for a light color with warm hues and a strong solution if dark colors are desired (for a medium solution, most suggest mixing 1 pea-size nugget for about every 1 cup of water).

Once the desired color is achieved, rinse off the pieces in cold water. To stop further oxidation, dip the pieces in a weak solution (1:4) of baking soda and water.

Don't be afraid to dip the metal pieces several times in the solution; they can always be lightened later by buffing or polishing, and sometimes unexpected colors, including purple, will appear after several dips. The solution does not maintain its potency so if you are going to dip pieces several times, it's best to do so in the same setting; otherwise, you'll need to mix a new batch of solution.

Hard-boiled egg: If you are adverse to the toxicity of patina and liver of sulfur, you can jump-start the natural oxidation process of sterling silver and copper using a hard-boiled egg.

Hard-boil an egg until cooked (about 10 to 15 minutes), place it in a container with an air-tight lid while still warm, and smash it a few times.

Hang the metal piece to be colored above the egg so that it does not have direct contact. To do so, string the piece onto thread, tape one end of the thread to each side of the container's rim, and place the lid on the container. Color typically develops within 24 to 36 hours. Repeat entire process if a deeper color is desired.

PAINTING METALS

To give metal pieces a patinated look without using chemicals, try acrylic crafter's paint. Available at craft stores, this paint can be applied to metal surfaces with a foam brush, then buffed, if desired, with extra-fine steel wool.

caring for metals

You can almost guarantee that all metals will change color with age. Here are a few ways to restore a metal's original shine and prevent discoloration, starting with general rules that apply to all metals:

ALL METALS

+ Jewelry should be the last thing on and the first thing you take off to reduce exposing metals to beauty products such as perfume, hairspray, cosmetics, and lotion.

+ Think of jewelry as a living material; it is sensitive to extreme temperatures, humidity, chemicals, and harsh sunlight.

+ Don't wear your favorite pieces when it's hot out or when exercising; sweat can wreak havoc on most metals.

+ All jewelry can be damaged by household chemicals. Remove your jewels or wear gloves when cleaning house and definitely don't wear them in a swimming pool or hot tub.

+ The higher the content of pure metal, the less likely it is to tarnish: For example, Thai silver is less prone to tarnishing than sterling silver because it has a higher silver content—it's the alloys in metals, like copper, that encourage tarnish.

+ You can find a commercial cleaner for almost any metal—you'll be surprised by the selection. But realize that cleaning products can discolor beads, especially stones, so be sure to carefully read the cleaner's label.

+ Regardless of the product you choose, always be sure the cloth or pair of gloves you use to wipe and buff the jewelry is soft and non-abrasive (100 percent cotton is preferred).

+ If the item being cleaned already has a brushed satin finish, you can safely use a bristle brush to remove stubborn discoloring.

+ When all else fails, take your jewelry to a restoration specialist for professional help.

+ When you find heavy areas of oxidation, whether black or green, follow this rule: clean it, buff it, then protect it against future damage.

+ Though your jewelry box will no longer look like a sunken treasure chest, it is best to keep silver and base metals safely tucked away in plastic bags (however jewelry with pearls should not be stored this way as pearls tend to turn brittle and crack if kept too dry).

+ Clean hollow items by buffing them—if you dip them in a cleaning solution or soapy water, you run the risk of not being able to fully flush out the cleaning material.

GOLD

+ Though gold is the only metal that does not tarnish in its pure state, it can still look soiled. To easily restore shine, it is safe to clean gold using warm water and a mild detergent, being sure to thoroughly dry the pieces immediately after washing and follow up with a polishing cloth. Before washing gold, Mark Moeller, of R. F. Moeller Jewelers, suggests dipping gold jewelry in plain rubbing alcohol or vodka to remove oily buildup.

SILVER

+ Because silver is sensitive to moisture, it will tarnish more rapidly in humid climates. To absorb excess moisture, keep a packet of silica gel desiccant (the moisture-removing packets often found in shoeboxes) in the same container you store jewelry. To reduce exposure to oxygen and moisture, store silver in tightly sealed plastic bags. And for even better protection, first wrap pieces in acid-free, antitarnish tissue.

+ When silver does tarnish, there are a handful of products—from polishing creams, cloths, and gloves to liquid rinses—that will restore its original finish. Cleaners containing synthetic wax are to be avoided as they may leave a residue.

For the materials listed in this book, check your local bead shop or contact the companies listed here (see pp. 107–108 for contact information). Remember, some beads and findings, both new and vintage, are limited in availability; if the companies don't have the exact beads shown in this book, they'll probably have something similar that will work just as well.

project resources

gold

ROSY POSIES
by Danielle Fox

Head pins, clasp, jump rings, chain, and wire: Shiana. Ring: The Bead Goes On.

GRETA GARBO
by Melinda Barta

Clasps: The Whole Bead Shop. Beading wire: Beadalon (wholesale only). Chain: Artbeads.com. All other beads and findings: FusionBeads.com.

FIRST LADY
by Melinda Barta

Pearls, crimp tubes, and crimp covers: FusionBeads.com. Gold rounds, coins, button beads, pendants, head pins, and clasp: The Whole Bead Shop. Ribbon: Jo-Ann Fabric and Craft. Beading wire: Beadalon (wholesale only). Ear wires: Shiana.

GOLDEN BLUSH
by Danielle Fox

All beads: North Star Jewelry Supply. Flat oval rings, clasp, chain, and wire: FusionBeads.com. Jump ring: Via Murano.

silver

GHOST RANCH *by Melinda Barta*
Beach glass, pendant, and all fine silver: Zoa Art. Hammered chain and 14mm round charm: Kamol (wholesale only). Patterned chain: Shiana. Clasp: Green Girl Studios. Wire and jump rings: FusionBeads.com. Aquamarine rondelles: Desert Gems.

SILVER SHADE *by Melinda Barta*
Quartz: Desert Gems. Beading wire: Beadalon (wholesale only). Crimp tubes and crimp covers: FusionBeads .com. All other silver beads and findings: The Whole Bead Shop.

SILVER LINING *by Danielle Fox*
Mystic sapphire teardrop: Wraps, Stones & Things. Diamond and "soar" charms, wing pendant, hammered ring, clasp, and large chain: Nina Designs. Long teardrop charm, small chain, 6mm jump rings, and wire: FusionBeads.com. 4mm jump rings: Via Murano.

SILVERED BUDS *by Danielle Fox*
Pressed-glass flowers: Raven's Journey International. Thai silver rondelles: Kamol (wholesale only). Thai silver charms, flower bead, and puffed squares: Niki Passenier. Head pins, crimp tubes, and crimp covers:

Fire Mountain Gems and Beads. Ear wires: Rishashay. Wire: Soft Flex Co.

base metals

BLOOMS IN BRASS *by Melinda Barta*
Rhodonite, jade, and pale blue rounds: Beadz. Antique brass jump rings, connecter, hammered rings, and G-S Hypo Cement: Ornamentea. Craft wire and natural brass jump rings, head pins, toggle bar, toggle ring, and bead caps: FusionBeads.com.

LUCK, LOVE & COPPER
by Danielle Fox

Copper hearts and rounds: Papio Creek Gems & Gifts. Copper rings and ear wires: Earth 2 Sea Designs. Pendant: Kismet Designs. Clasp, chain, and wire: FusionBeads.com. Jump rings: Via Murano.

BRONZE BEAUTY *by Danielle Fox*
Seed beads: Beyond Beadery. Pressed-glass rectangles: Bokamo Designs. Bronze bracelet finding and charms: Crystals & Dreams/Star Spirit Studio. Lobster clasp: AD Adornments. Crimp beads, ear wires, and craft wire: Ornamentea. Beading wire: Beadalon (wholesale only).

project resources, *continued*

LYRICAL LARIAT *by Melinda Barta*
Jump rings: Ornamentea. Chain and wire: FusionBeads.com. Charms and connectors: Green Girl Studios. Irregular ring: Shiana.

WE ♥ PEWTER *by Melinda Barta*
Pearls: Saki Silver. Swarovski crystals: The Beadin' Path. Hammered chain: Kamol (wholesale only). Round 3mm and rollo chain: Bead Cache. Pewter: Green Girl Studios. Round 6mm chain: Beading House. Beading and sterling silver wire, crimp tubes, crimp covers, and head pins: FusionBeads.com.

faux metals

FOOL FOR GOLD *by Melinda Barta*
Round chain, fire-polished rounds, pressed-glass rounds, pyrite, and rhodonite: Beadz. Oval chains and jump rings: Ornamentea. Head pins, bead caps, crystals, crimp tubes, and crimp covers: FusionBeads.com. Clasp: The Beadin' Path. Sequins: Gail Crosman Moore. Finished teardrop dangles, lampworked drops, clear/peach mottled round, and pressed-glass-flower dangle: French General. Beading wire: Beadalon (wholesale only).

COMET & CUPID *by Danielle Fox*
Swarovski crystal rounds: Beyond Beadery. Vintage Swarovski crystal flowers: The Beadin' Path. Clasp: Fire Mountain Gems and Beads. Wire-lace ribbon, head pins, crimp tubes, and

crimp covers: FusionBeads.com. Beading wire: Beadalon (wholesale only).

GILDED GARLAND *by Melinda Barta*
Clasp: Jess Imports (wholesale only). Gold and clear rounds: Aloha Bead Co. Blue flowers: Raven's Journey International. Clear flowers: Bokamo Designs. Wire, crimp tubes, and crimp covers: FusionBeads.com.

ENAMEL AMOUR *by Danielle Fox*
Vintage enamel flowers: Sleeping Dog Studio. Vintage enamel chain: Epoch Beads. Epoxy-coated ovals: Fire Mountain Gems and Beads. Rhinestone round and jump rings: Ornamentea. Clasp: The Beadin' Path. Head pin and daisy spacer: FusionBeads.com.

mixing metals

FEATHER YOUR NEST *by Danielle Fox*
Seed beads: Jane's Fiber and Beads. Pearls: Talisman Associates. Lampworked eggs: Karen Elmquist. Antique glass rings: Bead Paradise II. "Good egg" photo charm: Vintage Faerie. Natural brass bird charms, spacers, bead caps, head pins, and jump rings: FusionBeads.com. Bird-print rounds and toggle clasp: Green Girl Studios. Sterling silver nest and bird beads: Elemental Adornments. Maple leaf charms: Niki Passenier. Egg-and-nest links: Hip Chick Beads. Raw

brass bird links and bird cutout charm: Dava Bead and Trade. Sterling silver jump rings: Via Murano. Antique brass jump rings and craft wire: Ornamentea. Chain: AD Adornments.

ADORNING APHRODITE *by Melinda Barta*
Lucite rounds and bead caps: Chelsea's Beads. Clasp and Lucite ovals: The Beadin' Path. Pendant: Jennifer Morris Beads & Jewelry. Crystals, crimp tubes, and crimp covers: FusionBeads.com. Jump ring: Ornamentea. Beading wire: Beadalon (wholesale only).

SECRET GARDEN *by Melinda Barta*
Wire and chain: Antelope Beads. Pearls: Saki Silver. Pendant, clasp, and rings: Elemental Adornments. Bead caps and jump rings: FusionBeads .com. Hook clasp: Susan Lenart Kazmer.

MEMORIES OF VICTORIA *by Danielle Fox*
Pressed-glass rounds: I Fancy That! Fire-polished rondelles and pressed-glass flowers: Raven's Journey International. Mottled glass rounds: Bokamo Designs. Finished dangles and filigree charms: Stone Mountain Colorado. Copper teardrops: Papio Creek Gems & Gifts. Brass locket and craft wire: Ornamentea. Filigree rounds, feather charms, lobster clasp, head pins, and chain: AD Adornments. Bead caps, jump rings, spacers/crimp covers, crimp tubes, and beading wire: FusionBeads.com.

Check your local bead shop or contact the companies below to purchase the materials used in this book. Remember that suppliers may have limited quantities, so don't hesitate to substitute your own favorite beads and findings for the featured materials. See p. 105 for a resource guide to each project.

start shopping

materials

AD ADORNMENTS
kathyd33@yahoo.com
adadornments.com

ALOHA BEAD CO.
43 Hana Hwy.
Paia, HI 96779
(808) 579-9709

ANTELOPE BEADS
PO Box 547
Boulder, CO 80306
(303) 447-0725
antelopebeads.com

ARTBEADS.COM
11901 137th Ave. Ct. KPN,
Unit 100
Gig Harbor, WA 98329
(866) 715-2323
artbeads.com

BEAD CACHE
3307 S. College Ave., Unit 105
Fort Collins, CO 80525
(970) 224-4322

BEAD GOES ON, THE
2700 Avenger Dr., Ste. 111
Virginia Beach, VA 23452
(866) 861-2323
beadgoeson.com

BEAD PARADISE II
29 W. College St.
Oberlin, OH 44074
(440) 775-2233
beadparadise.com

**BEADALON
(wholesale only)**
440 Highlands Blvd.
Coatesville, PA 19320
(866) 423-2325
beadalon.com

BEADIN' PATH, THE
15 Main St.
Freeport, ME 04032
(877) 922-3237
beadinpath.com

BEADING HOUSE
(425) 652-9652
beadinghouse.com

BEADZ
324 Walnut St.
Fort Collins, CO 80524
(970) 224-2572

BEYOND BEADERY
PO Box 460
Rollinsville, CO 80474
(800) 840-5548
beyondbeadery.com

BOKAMO DESIGNS
5609 W. 99th St.
Overland Park, KS 66207
(913) 648-4296
bokamodesigns.com

CHELSEA'S BEADS
1799 St. Johns Ave.
Highland Park, IL 60035
(847) 433-3451
chelseasbeads.com

**CRYSTALS & DREAMS/
STAR SPIRIT STUDIO**
PO Box 141
Guffey, CO 80820
(719) 689-3101
beadandgemstoneimport.com

DAVA BEAD & TRADE
2121 NE Broadway
Portland, OR 97232
(503) 288-3991
davabeadandtrade.com

DESERT GEMS
457 Wadsworth Blvd.
Lakewood, CO 80226
(303) 426-4411
desertgemsinc.com

EARTH 2 SEA DESIGNS
e2ssupplies.etsy.com

**ELEMENTAL
ADORNMENTS**
(319) 364-0658
christi.anderson
@elementaladornments.com
elementaladornments.com

EPOCH BEADS
epochbeads.etsy.com

**FIRE MOUNTAIN
GEMS AND BEADS**
1 Fire Mountain Wy.
Grants Pass, OR 97526
(800) 355-2137
firemountaingems.com

FRENCH GENERAL
1621 Vista Del Mar Ave.
Hollywood, CA 90028
(323) 462-0818
frenchgeneral.com

FUSIONBEADS.COM
3830 Stone Wy. N.
Seattle, WA 98103
(888) 781-3559
fusionbeads.com

GAIL CROSMAN MOORE
71 Creamery Hill Rd.
North Orange, MA 01364
gail@ gailcrosmanmoore.com
gailcrosmanmoore.com

GREEN GIRL STUDIOS
PO Box 19389
Asheville, NC 28815
(828) 298-2263
www.greengirlstudios.com

HIP CHICK BEADS
4414 160th Cir.
Urbandale, IA 50323
(515) 771-8600
www.hipchickbeads.com

I FANCY THAT!
(303) 470-7695
ifancythat@comcast.net

JANE'S FIBER & BEADS
PO Box 110
5415 E. Andrew Johnson Hwy.
Afton, TN 37616
(888) 497-2665
www.janesfiberandbeads.com

JENNIFER MORRIS BEADS & JEWELRY
www.jennifermorrisbeads.
etsy.com

JESS IMPORTS
(wholesale only)
110 Gough St., Ste. 203A
San Francisco, CA 94102
(415) 626-1433
www.jessimports.com

JO-ANN FABRIC AND CRAFT
(888) 739-4120
www.joann.com

KAMOL
(wholesale only)
PO Box 95619
Seattle, WA 98145
(206) 764-7375
info@kamol.com
www.kamol.com

KAREN ELMQUIST
http://stores.ebay.com/
Miss- Spiders-Web

KISMET DESIGNS
www.kismetdesigns.etsy.com
www.kismetdesigns.biz

NIKI PASSENIER
PO Box 1744
Albany, OR 97321
nikipassenier@gmail.com

NINA DESIGNS
PO Box 8127
Emeryville, CA 94662
(800) 336-6462
www.ninadesigns.com

NORTH STAR JEWELRY SUPPLY
4680 Broadway St.
Boulder, CO 80304
(303) 442-2577
www.nsjewelrysupply.com

ORNAMENTEA
509 N. West St.
Raleigh, NC 27603
(919) 834-6260
www.ornamentea.com

PAPIO CREEK GEMS & GIFTS
8056 S. 84th St.
La Vista, NE 68128
(402) 935-4367
pcgems@jagwireless.net
www.papiobeads.com

RAVEN'S JOURNEY INTERNATIONAL
PO Box 3099
Port Angeles, WA 98362
sales@theravenstore.com
www.theravenstore.com

RISHASHAY
PO Box 8271
Missoula, MT 59807
(800) 517-3311
www.rishashay.com

SAKI SILVER
3268 Jefferson Ave.
Cincinnati, OH 45220
(513) 221-5480
www.sakisilver.com

SHIANA
www.shiana.com

SLEEPING DOG STUDIO
www.sleepingdogstudio.
etsy.com
www.wendybakerdesign.com

SOFT FLEX COMPANY
PO Box 80
Sonoma, CA 95476
(707) 938-3539
www.softflexcompany.com

STONE MOUNTAIN COLORADO
PO Box 1250
Walsenburg, CO 81089
(719) 738-3991

SUSAN LENART KAZMER
23216 E. Echo Lake Rd.
Snohomish, WA 98296
(206) 910-8243
www.susanlenartkazmer.net

TALISMAN ASSOCIATES
2001-A Veirs Mill Rd.
Rockville, MD 20851
(800) 229-7890
www.tailsmanbeads.com

VIA MURANO
17654 Newhope St., Ste. A
Fountain Valley, CA 92708
(877) VIAMURANO
www.viamurano.com

VINTAGE FAERIE
PO Box 853
Mendenhall, PA 19357
info@vintagefaerie.com
www.vintagefaerie.com

WRAPS, STONES & THINGS
888 Brannon St., Ste. 602
San Francisco, CA 94103
(415) 863-4953
www.beadsnclasps.com

WHOLE BEAD SHOP, THE
PO Box 1100
Nevada City, CA 95959
(800) 796-5350
www.wholebeadshop.com

ZOA ART
zoaart@yahoo.com
www.zoaart.com

magazines

BEADWORK
beadworkmagazine.com

STEP BY STEP BEADS
stepbystepbeads.com

STEP BY STEP WIRE JEWELRY
stepbystepwirejewelry.com

STRINGING
stringingmagazine.com

websites
interweave.com
beadingdaily.com
www.etsy.com

bead shows
beadfest.com
wirejewelryfest.com

index & bibliography

bibliography

BOOKS

Charron, Shirley. *Modern Pewter Design and Techniques.* New York: Van Nostrand Reinhold Co., 1973.

Mason, Anita and Diane Packer. *An Illustrated Dictionary of Jewellery.* New York: Harper & Row, Publishers, 1974.

Sarett, Morton R. *The Jewelry in Your Life.* Chicago: Nelson-Hall, 1979.

Schiffer, Peter, Nancy, and Herbert. *The Brass Book: American, English and European, Fifteenth Century through 1850.* Exton, Pennsylvania: Schiffer Publishing Co., 1978.

Tait, Hugh. *Jewelry: 7,000 Years.* New York: Harry N. Abrams, 1986.

World Book Encyclopedia. Chicago: World Book, 2008.

WEBSITES

Copper Development Association, copper.org.

The Silver Institute, silverinstitute.org.

World Gold Council, gold.org.

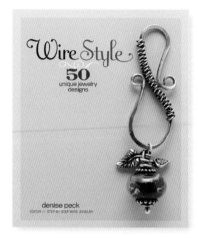